See pg. 118 Prayer of the heart
125 Ca
181 Eucharist Life
189 Coming Home to Jesus
(on dying)

Doris Stollsteimer
9 Dunbarton RD
Jackson NJ 08527

The Only Necessary Thing

HENRI J.M. NOUWEN

The Only Necessary Thing

LIVING A PRAYERFUL LIFE

EDITED BY
WENDY WILSON GREER

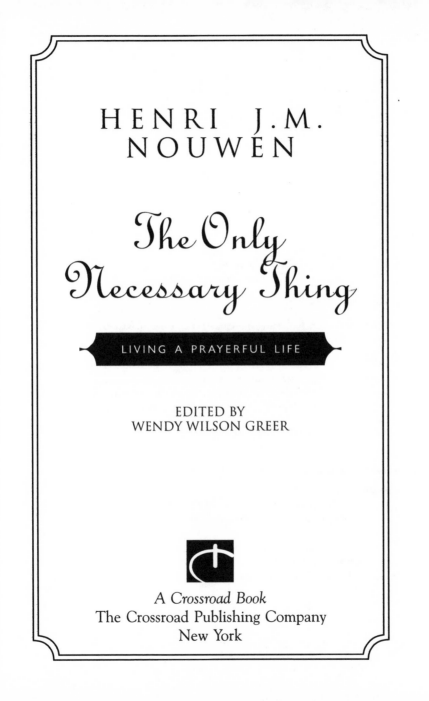

A Crossroad Book
The Crossroad Publishing Company
New York

The Crossroad Publishing Company
370 Lexington Avenue, New York, NY 10017

Printed in the United States of America

Library of Congress Cataloging-in-Publication Data
Nouwen, Henri J. M.
   The only necessary thing : living a prayerful life / Henri J.M.
Nouwen ; compiled and edited by Wendy Wilson Greer.
      p.   cm.
   Includes bibliographical references.
   ISBN 0-8245-1833-0 (hc.)
   1. Prayer – Catholic Church.   I. Greer, Wendy Wilson.   II. Title.
BV210.2 .N65   1999
248.3′2 – dc21   99-43205

4   5   6   7   8   9   10   04   03   02   01

For Henri,
dear friend and inspiring teacher,
with deepest gratitude

&

For Jay,
my beloved husband and partner in prayer,
with dearest love

Contents

7

Foreword

Entering the Dayspring house late one afternoon I came upon Henri drinking coffee and in tears. "What happened?" I asked anxiously.

"Oh, I had a bump today that upset me more than usual," he answered dejectedly. "This morning, as I always do, I was rushing to get to the Council Meeting, and Dan stopped me and wanted to speak to me. I guess I was preoccupied because I quickly said I couldn't see him. A few minutes ago he telephoned and gave me a piece of his mind. He was angry and he said that I preached beautiful theories about the Christian life that I never lived up to, and that I, supposedly a man of prayer, was selfish and rude. His remarks surprised me and caught me off guard. They were hurtful, especially because they were true." Henri and I talked for a while and later, as he prepared to leave, he said something that stayed with me and consoled me. "I wonder," he pondered, "if Dan ever considered what I would be like if I wasn't a man of prayer?"

Henri was indeed a man of prayer. He loved his priesthood, and he loved to celebrate the Eucharist each day. When he taught in the university, he invited students, individually and in groups, to pray with him. During the last ten years, he and I, with others, began our day at 6:30 a.m. in our small, "Dayspring" chapel. We prayed silently for half an hour before reciting together Morning Prayer from the Liturgy of the Hours in the Divine Office. Henri loved reading those Psalms in the Prayer of the Church, knowing that he was doing so in unison with thousands of lay people, monks, nuns, and clergy worldwide who prayed the same Morning Prayer. Late in the afternoon and before supper when we were both home we again took the Office book to recite Evening Prayer. And often, if we happened to meet before retiring, we read Night Prayer as well. Whoever happened to be present was invited by Henri to pray with us because he liked to pray with others. He could preach a whole sermon on the value of being "alone together" in prayer. In difficult meetings, in consultation sessions, and at the end of a gathering, Henri was the one to invite us all to pray together before going our separate ways.

Almost all of Henri's books refer to his personal, life-long struggle to give space and time to the One who longed to communicate with him in solitude. He learned to pray at his mother's knee, and through school and seminary, through travel, teaching, and lecturing, he never lost his sense that prayer was a necessity for him. His writings about prayer spring not from his mind but from his experience of longing for God, of sometimes experiencing the "Presence" and of often being challenged to hope in the darkness. Prayer was the growing edge of a spiritual journey that led him far, wide, and deep into the experience of claiming himself as a Beloved Child of God. This inner Communion with God was for him dynamic, challenging, comforting, always changing, and forever opening in him new experiences of and insights into the world of love.

Henri grew more and more articulate about the ways of God and our human response as his life progressed. Thus, when Wendy Greer approached me about a Henri Nouwen Reader on the topic of prayer, I was somewhat skeptical. I wondered if the passages she spoke of, especially from older books, wouldn't be a bit "yellow around the edges." They were, in my opinion, no match for the living words that came in Henri's later years. I imagined that Wendy's labor might result in a heavy "tome" fit only for researchers, scholars, and theologians.

I could not have been more wrong!

You see, Wendy didn't have to research this book. She, her husband, Jay, and her children, Kate, Heather, and Jonathan, had always worshiped God and prayed together as a family. Wendy herself was on a personal journey to become a woman of prayer, and Henri had been her mentor on the way. She had long since not only marked many passages about prayer in each of Henri's books as part of her own spiritual quest, but had, herself, chosen prayer as a life-line for living. Wendy knew communion with God for many years, long before she ever conceived the notion of a book.

Thus, the book comes from Wendy's love of God, and from Wendy's love of Henri. The book is the fruit of her relationship with God as a beloved daughter. Wendy is masterful in gathering Henri's texts under such headings as: Solitude, Belovedness, Listening, Discipline, and Forgiveness, among others. The whole text flows beautifully, offering instruction and penetrating inspiration. This book is a deep and conscious act of love; dynamic, radiant, cohesive, and shining with excerpts of true wisdom and beauty. I believe this book on prayer is a classic!

The Only Necessary Thing begins with desire: ours for God and God's for us so that we enter immediately into a realm where intimate communication with God is responding to some profound aspirations of our hearts. On this new landscape we are called and challenged by the adventure of finding, in the Grand Canyon of our loneliness, the in-exhaustible source of love in our lives. "We are called to convert our loneliness into solitude. We are called to experi-ence our aloneness not as a wound but as a gift — as God's gift — so that in our aloneness we might discover how deeply we are loved by God" (see p. 43). But this does not happen quickly. We must go through the stages where feelings of love and hate, tenderness and pain, forgiveness and greed are sep-arated, strengthened, or reformed. Gradually, very gradually, we begin to "feel" the gentle hand of the loving Gardener who is working in our hearts.

This inner conversion and regulation of our hearts is about our very identity. Jesus at his baptism heard the voice that called him, "Beloved." This voice had a profound impact on him and allowed him to live always as the Chosen One of God. He was able to withstand the temptations of the devil in the desert, to stand before those who criticized him, and before those who killed him, not cowering, but free and aware of who he was and to whom he belonged. Henri urges us to claim ourselves as beloved children of a God who longs for our love. This is a whole new perspective on life. Do we dare to believe that a relationship of love and intimacy is possible between our God and ourselves? Henri helps us with the story of Jesus, the Jealous Lover, asking Peter three times, "Do you love me?" noting that Jesus waited, offering Peter endless opportunities for the response. "Prayer," says Henri, "is listening to that voice — to the One who calls you the Beloved" (p. 67).

The Only Necessary Thing offers us lessons on listening and on the disciplines necessary for the long journey of life toward our true and lasting home. In the short, clear, and concise passages, we recognize our own need to stop, reflect, and listen. We also know the inner "motor" that races and pushes us into activity and distraction. We identify with the texts describing our resistance to the practice of patience, while complaining about being distracted, busy, and exhausted. Henri encourages us. "When discipline keeps us faithful, we slowly begin to sense that something so deep, so mysterious, and so creative is happening here.... We experience the presence of the compassionate God" (p. 97). And "Let us not be discouraged," says Henri. "Jesus walks with us and speaks to us on the road. When we listen carefully we discover that we are already home while on the way" (p. 105).

Henri explains how solitude and prayer permeate our days. "The prayer of the heart ... is indeed like a murmuring stream that continues underneath the many waves of every day and opens the possibility of living in the world without being of it and of reaching out to our God from the center of our solitude" (p. 119).

The book captures Henri's insight into how solitude naturally leads us to community. It inspires us to take a true place in the human family where God's spirit of love moves us beyond time and space into a cosmic experience of belonging. "The community of love stretches out not only beyond the boundaries of countries and continents but also beyond the boundaries of decades and centuries. Not only the awareness of those who are far away but also the memory of those who lived long ago can lead us into a healing, sustaining, and guiding community. The space for God in community transcends all limits of time and place.... This is the real Pentecost experience" (p. 132).

Living a life of union with God in prayer does not lead us to despair, but rather to the joyful discovery that we are only human and that God is God. A fruit growing from a life of prayer is to experience the "embrace of a forgiving God" (p. 159)

Speaking of death and eternal life, Henri leads us to glimpse the reality of our approaching death, not as something fearful and traumatic, but more as a "return to the womb of God" (p. 190). Communion with God grows deep inside us and we gradually learn a trust so tangible that we begin to image our death as a "letting go" of the swing on the flying trapeze. Henri quotes the trapeze artist Rodleigh, who says, "When I fly to Joe, I have simply to stretch out my arms and hands and wait for him to catch me and pull me safely over the apron behind the catchbar.... The worst thing a flyer can do is to try to catch the catcher." "Dying is trusting the catcher," says Henri. "Don't try to grab Him; He will grab you. Just stretch out your arms and hands and trust, trust, trust" (pp. 195–96).

In the final section we have the unique privilege of praying with Henri. With a selection of published and unpublished prayers, we see the heart of the one who has been our instructor in the art of prayer. This is a needy, shaky, unsettled heart, yearning for intimacy and love. It is also a courageous, generous heart, willing to die a little "as a way of experiencing some solidarity with the millions in this world who suffer far more than I do" (p. 201). It isn't difficult for our hearts to identify with Henri's yearning heart. The prayers, so humble and simple, cover his teaching with authenticity.

Dan saw Henri as a man of prayer who should have been above the experience of human brokenness. Henri saw himself as a vulnerable but beloved child of God who, in

communion with the Beloved, knew transformation and salvation. *The Only Necessary Thing* exemplifies this experience,
not as unique, but as universal. What a hope for us and for
our world!

SUE MOSTELLER, C.S.J.

Henri Nouwen Literary Centre
Richmond Hill, Ontario, Canada
June 1, 1999

Preface

Henri Nouwen has been and continues to be a beloved spiritual guide to countless people around the world. He has been described in many ways: one of the most influential spiritual writers of the twentieth century, an icon of Western spirituality, a brilliant theologian, a prophet, a wounded healer, a powerful preacher, a man of the heart, and a faithful, generous friend, to name just a few. Like many people, I first met him through his books in the mid-1970s, and he became a soul mate almost immediately. Each book I read seemed to be written just for me, articulating the deepest desires of my heart.

Though I was deeply moved by Henri's books, it took me over fifteen years to write him a letter to express my gratitude. The final typed version of this letter was fifteen pages long — nearly a page for each year. A few weeks after mailing the letter, I received *The Return of the Prodigal Son* beautifully inscribed to me by Henri. This gift touched me profoundly (what I didn't know then was that he sent books to people like me all the time), and we began to correspond on a regular basis. I met him the following year at a conference in North Carolina, and a few weeks later he began staying with us in our apartment in New York City. He soon became one of my closest friends and one of our favorite visitors.

Henri, who had taught me for years through his books, began teaching me even more through his personal example on his frequent visits. No matter how tired he was when he came — and he was usually exhausted — he was always faithful to his prayer discipline. He frequently invited us to say Morning and Evening Prayers with him, and he celebrated the Eucharist with us whenever it was possible. When we visited him at L'Arche Daybreak, he always rose early and invited us to pray with him in the Dayspring chapel, and we often ended the day by saying Night Prayers with him.

What I remember most about praying with Henri is how his compassionate heart embraced the suffering world with a radical inclusivity. When he prayed with us, he would always begin by praying for our families, for his L'Arche community, and for close friends in need. Then his prayers would expand to include people all over the world: the sick and dying, the homeless and lonely, prisoners and refugees, people with AIDS, cancer, or mental illness, and victims of famine, war, or natural disasters. His prayers were very simple but very profound.

On several occasions I asked Henri to recommend books on prayer to me, but with one exception, he always said emphatically, "You learn to pray by praying!" So why did I compile a book by him on prayer? Over the years I had marked many passages on prayer in his books — passages that guided me on my own prayer journey. As I reflected on these selections after Henri's sudden death in 1996, I had a strong feeling that they were words of great wisdom, inspiration, and encouragement, not just for me, but for others as well. However, these quotes came from twenty-nine different books! With Sue Mosteller's permission, I have combined these excerpts with others I found specifically for this collection in one book as a resource for people who are seeking to live a prayerful life.

In *Reaching Out* Henri writes: "Among the many great spiritual men and women in history we may find a few, or maybe just one or two, who speak the language of our heart and give us courage. These are our guides. Not to be imitated but to help us live our lives just as authentically as they lived theirs. When we have found such guides we have good reason to be grateful and even better reasons to listen attentively to what they have to say."

Henri Nouwen has been an inspiring guide for me and for thousands of people around the world. He has certainly spoken and written "the language of our heart" and given many, many people courage. As a guide he is definitely a companion on the way, gently but persistently urging us to seek an ever closer relationship with God and his son, Jesus Christ. He had a contagious faith in Jesus and the ability to make him come alive today. The recurring theme of belovedness found in his works challenges each of us to live our lives as beloved sons and daughters of God. As we learn to claim our own belovedness through prayer, we will then come to see the belovedness in others.

What a great privilege and blessing it has been for me to know this man of prayer and to edit this book! I pray the readers of *The Only Necessary Thing* will "listen attentively" to Henri's words and, like me, find countless reasons to be deeply grateful for his unique guidance, wisdom, encouragement, authenticity, and above all, for his extravagant love of God.

WENDY WILSON GREER
President, Henri Nouwen Society

June 1999
New York City

Acknowledgments

I want to express my deep gratitude to the following people who have given me remarkable assistance and support:

Sue Mosteller, Henri's Literary Executrix, not only entrusted me with the compilation of this book but also generously read the manuscript and offered valuable suggestions. In addition, she gave me permission to include articles and unpublished prayers and, because Henri would have done so, to use inclusive language where needed. She also arranged to have my manuscript typed. My thanks to her are abundant.

Susan Brown used her considerable editing skills to hone the selection and organization of my original manuscript and to make the language more inclusive.

Catherine Cripps typed and retyped the manuscript capably and joyfully.

The Rev. Brenda Husson and Gil Vasquez at St. James' Church graciously allowed me to duplicate materials on the church photocopier on favorable terms.

Don McNeill, C.S.C., gave me a copy of *Henri Nouwen,* a collection of articles put together by the Center for Social Concerns at the University of Notre Dame.

Drew Theological School produced *The Nouwen Notebook,* with articles compiled by Michael J. Christensen and Carl E. Savage, for participants of the 1997 Tipple-Vosburg Lectures.

Martha Smalley and her staff at the Special Collections Department of the Yale Divinity School Library, made it possible for me to look through dozens of articles in the Nouwen Collection efficiently.

Gwendolin Herder and Bob Heller welcomed me warmly to Crossroad Publishing Company and gave me encouragement and very helpful advice. They were remarkably open to my ideas about everything from the content and organization of this book to its title and cover. Christine Gunn did a wonderful job securing the necessary permissions.

Many friends have prayed with me over the years and have been reflections of God's love. Although I am unable to list their names, I am thankful for each of them. I must single our my parents, Brownlow and Joy Wilson, who introduced me to prayer at an early age and lived prayerful lives. I am deeply grateful for their love and example.

I have been truly blessed by the love and support of my family. My children, Kate, Heather, and Jonathan, have followed the progress of this book with keen interest. My husband, Jay, has wholeheartedly loved and supported me and good-naturedly accepted the disorganization in our home that resulted from my preoccupation with this project. He is my companion on the way, wise counselor, and dearest friend; his beautiful prayers nurture my soul.

And, finally, my deepest gratitude goes to Henri Nouwen. His shining example, beautiful words, and loving spirit have guided me throughout this endeavor. More than anyone else, he has shown me and continues to show me how to live a prayerful life.

The Only Necessary Thing

An Invitation

The invitation to a life of prayer is the invitation to live in the midst of this world without being caught in the net of wounds and needs. The word "prayer" stands for a radical interruption of the vicious chain of interlocking dependencies leading to violence and war and for an entering into a totally new dwelling place. It points to a new way of speaking, a new way of breathing, a new way of being together, a new way of knowing, yes, a whole new way of living.

It is not easy to express the radical change that prayer represents, since for many the word "prayer" is associated with piety, talking to God, thinking about God, morning and evening exercises, Sunday services, grace before meals, sentences from the Bible, and many other things. All of these have something to do with prayer, but when I speak about prayer...I speak first of all about moving away from the dwelling place of those who hate peace into the house of God....Prayer is the center of the Christian life. *It is the only necessary thing* (Luke 10:42). It is living with God here and now.
— "Prayer and Peacemaking"

One

Desire

Our desire for God is the desire that should guide all other desires.

— *Bread for the Journey*

The more we pray — in the sense of living a prayerful life — the more we desire to pray.

— "Prayer and Ministry"

The Desire to Pray

The more we pray — in the sense of living a prayerful life —
the more we desire to pray. If we live a prayerful life, then
there is a growing desire to spend more time with God and
God alone. It is always the opposite of what people think. It
is not, "Oh, my life is prayer so I don't have to say prayers."
Rather, the desire to pray and to spend time with God and
God alone is always growing. It creates in us a desire to be
with the Lord whom we have seen shining through people
and events, to be with the Lord alone. Then prayer becomes
one of the greatest gifts that we can have, because to be
with God whom we discover during the day, to be with God
and God alone is a great desire. It is as though you have
worked with your friends all day, but in the evening it is nice
to be with them and them alone, just to be with these special
people.   — "Prayer and Ministry"

Our Desire for God

Desire is often talked about as something we ought to overcome. Still, being is desiring: our bodies, our minds, our
hearts, and our souls are full of desires. Some are unruly,
turbulent, and very distracting; some make us think deep
thoughts and see great visions; some teach us how to love;
and some keep us searching for God. Our desire for God
is the desire that should guide all other desires. Otherwise
our bodies, minds, hearts, and souls become one another's
enemies and our inner lives become chaotic, leading us to
despair and self-destruction.

Spiritual disciplines are not ways to eradicate all our desires but ways to order them so that they can serve one another and together serve God.   — *Bread for the Journey*

The Treasure of God's Love

You have found a treasure: the treasure of God's love. You know now where it is, but you are not yet ready to own it fully. So many attachments keep pulling you away. If you would fully own your treasure, you must hide it in the field where you found it, go off happily to sell everything you own, and then come back and buy the field.

You can be truly happy that you have found the treasure. But you should not be so naïve as to think that you already own it. . . . Having found the treasure puts you on a new quest for it. The spiritual life is a long and often arduous search for what you have already found. You can seek God only when you have already found God. The desire for God's unconditional love is the fruit of having been touched by that love.

Because finding the treasure is only the beginning of the search, you have to be careful. If you expose the treasure to others without fully owning it, you might harm yourself and even lose the treasure. A newfound love needs to be nurtured in a quiet, intimate space. Overexposure kills it. . . . Finding the treasure without being ready yet to fully own it will make you restless. This is the restlessness of the search for God. It is the way to holiness. It is the road to the kingdom. It is the journey to the place where you can rest.

                                        — *The Inner Voice of Love*

God's Desire for Us

I am deeply convinced that the necessity to pray, and to pray
unceasingly, is not so much based on our desire for God as
on God's desire for us. It is God's passionate pursuit of us
that calls us to prayer. Prayer comes from God's initiative,
not ours. It might sound shocking, but it is biblical to say:
God wants us more than we want God! The English spiritual
writer Anthony Bloom (Metropolitan Anthony of Sourozh)
says it better than I when he writes:

> We complain that God does not make himself present
> to us for the few minutes we reserve for him, but what
> about the twenty-three and a half hours during which
> God may be knocking at our door and we answer, "I
> am busy. I am sorry." Or when we do not answer at all
> because we do not even hear the knock at the door of
> our heart, of our mind, of our conscience, of our life.
> So there is a situation in which we have no right to
> complain of the absence of God, because we are a great
> deal more absent than he ever is.

So, who is more in need of our prayers: we or God? God
is. Who wants to be heard most: we or God? God does. And
who "suffers" more from our lack of prayer: we or God? I say
it in awe but without fear: God does. As long as we continue
to reduce prayer to occasional piety we keep running away
from the mystery of God's jealous love, the love in which we
are created, redeemed, and made holy.

— "Prayer and the Jealous God"

Our Desire for Communion

What do we really desire? As I try to listen to my own deepest yearning as well as to the yearnings of others, the word that seems best to summarize the desire of the human heart is "communion." Communion means "union with." God has given us a heart that will remain restless until it has found full communion. We look for it in friendship, in marriage, in community. We look for it in sexual intimacy, in moments of ecstasy, in the recognition of our gifts. We look for it through success, admiration, and rewards. But wherever we look, it is communion we seek....

The desire for communion...is a God-given desire, a desire that causes immense pain as well as immense joy. Jesus came to proclaim that our desire for communion is not in vain, but will be fulfilled by the One who gave us that desire. The passing moments of communion are only hints of the Communion that God has promised us. The real danger facing us is to distrust our desire for communion. It is a God-given desire without which our lives lose their vitality and our hearts grow cold. A truly spiritual life is life in which we won't rest until we have found rest in the embrace of the One who is the Father and Mother of all desires.

— Here and Now

Two

What Is Prayer?

A spiritual life without prayer is like the Gospel without Christ.
                                        — *Reaching Out*

To pray . . . means to think and live in the presence of God.
                                        — *Clowning in Rome*

Reaching Out to God

Don't we use the word "prayer" mostly when we feel that our human limits are reached? Isn't the word "prayer" more a word to indicate powerlessness rather than a creative contact with the source of all life?

It is important to say that... feelings, experiences, questions, and irritations about prayer are very real and often the result of concrete and painful events. Still, a spiritual life without prayer is like the Gospel without Christ. Instead of proving or defending anything, it might be worthwhile to simply bring all the doubtful and anxious questions together in this one question: "If prayer, understood as an intimate relationship with God, is indeed the basis of all relationships — to ourselves as well as to others — how then can we learn to pray and really experience prayer as the axis of our existence?" By focusing on this question, it becomes possible to explore the importance of prayer in our own lives and in the lives of those we have met through personal encounters or through stories and books.

•

Prayer is often considered a weakness, a support system, which is used when we can no longer help ourselves. But this is only true when the God of our prayers is created in our own image and adapted to our own needs and concerns. When, however, prayer makes us reach out to God, not on our own but on God's terms, then prayer pulls us away from self-preoccupations, encourages us to leave familiar ground, and challenges us to enter into a new world which cannot be contained within the narrow boundaries of our mind or heart. Prayer, therefore, is a great adventure because the God with whom we enter into a new relationship is greater than we are and defies all our calculations and predictions. The movement from illusion to prayer is hard to make since it leads us from false certainties to true uncertainties, from an easy support system to a risky surrender, and from the many "safe" gods to the God whose love has no limits.

— *Reaching Out*

Dwelling in Jesus

Jesus leaves little doubt about the meaning of prayer when he says: "Apart from me you can do nothing; those who dwell in me as I dwell in them, bear much fruit" (John 15:5). Dwelling in Jesus is what prayer is all about.

Life becomes an unbearable burden whenever we lose touch with the presence of a loving Savior and see only hunger to be alleviated, injustice to be addressed, violence to be overcome, wars to be stopped, and loneliness to be removed. All these are critical issues, and Christians must try to solve them; however, when our concern no longer flows from our personal encounter with the living Christ, we feel oppressive weight.

Most of us try to get out from underneath by saying: "I have enough problems in keeping my own family and work going. Please do not burden me with the problems of the world. They only make me feel guilty and remind me of my powerlessness." We no longer participate in the full human reality, choosing instead to isolate ourselves in that corner of the world where we feel relatively safe. We may still say our fearful prayers, but we have forgotten that true prayer embraces the whole world, not just the small part where we live.

— "Prayer Embraces the World"

The Divine Spirit Praying in Us

The practice of contemplative prayer is the discipline by which we begin to see God in our heart. It is a careful attentiveness to the One who dwells in the center of our being such that through the recognition of God's presence we allow God to take possession of all our senses. Through the discipline of prayer we awaken ourselves to the God in us and let God enter into our heartbeat and our breathing, into our thoughts and emotions, our hearing, seeing, touching, and tasting. It is by being awake to this God in us that we can see God in the world around us. The great mystery of the contemplative life is not that we see God in the world, but that God within us recognizes God in the world. God speaks to God, Spirit speaks to Spirit, heart speaks to heart. Contemplation, therefore, is a participation in this divine self-recognition. It is the divine Spirit praying in us who makes our world transparent and opens our eyes to the presence of the divine Spirit in all that surrounds us. It is with our heart of hearts that we see the heart of the world. This explains the intimate relationship between contemplation and ministry. — *Clowning in Rome*

Prayer is the bridge between my unconscious and conscious life. Prayer connects my mind with my heart, my will with my passions, my brain with my belly. Prayer is the way to let the life-giving Spirit of God penetrate all the corners of my being. Prayer is the divine instrument of my wholeness, unity, and inner peace.

— *Sabbatical Journey*

Prayer and Suffering

"Come to me," Jesus says, "all you who are weary and find life burdensome, and I will refresh you. Take my yoke upon your shoulders and learn from me, for I am gentle and humble of heart. Your soul will find rest, for my yoke is easy, and my burden is light" (Matt. 12:29–30).

Here the deeper meaning of prayer becomes manifest. To pray is to unite ourselves with Jesus and lift up the whole world through him to God in a cry for forgiveness, reconciliation, healing, and mercy. To pray, therefore, is to connect whatever human struggle or pain we encounter — whether starvation, torture, displacement of peoples, or any form of physical and mental anguish — with the gentle and humble heart of Jesus....

Prayer is leading every sorrow to the source of all healing; it is letting the warmth of Jesus' love melt the cold anger of resentment; it is opening a space where joy replaces sadness, mercy supplants bitterness, love displaces fear, gentleness and care overcome hatred and indifference. But most of all, prayer is the way to become and remain part of Jesus' mission to draw all people to the intimacy of God's love.

— "Prayer Embraces the World"

Finding My Way to Pray

There are many ways to pray. When we are serious about prayer and no longer consider it one of the many things people do in their lives but, rather, the basic receptive attitude out of which all of life can receive new vitality, we will, sooner or later, raise the question: "What is *my* way to pray, what is the prayer of my heart?" Just as artists search for the style that is most their own, so people who pray search for the prayer of their heart. What is most profound in life, and therefore most dear to us, always needs to be properly protected as well as expressed. It, therefore, is not surprising that prayer is often surrounded by carefully prescribed gestures and words, by detailed rituals and elaborate ceremonies.

— Reaching Out

To Whom Do I Pray?

Speaking about prayer, I asked John Eudes a question that seemed very basic and a little naïve: "When I pray, to whom do I pray?" "When I say 'Lord,' what do I mean?"

John Eudes responded very differently than I expected. He said, "This is the real question, this is the most important question you can raise; at least this is the question that you can make your most important question." He stressed with great and convincing emphasis that if I really wanted to take the question seriously, I should realize that there would be little room left for other things. "Except," he said smiling, "when the question exhausts you so much that you need to read *Newsweek* for a little relaxation!" "It is far from easy," John Eudes said, "to make that question the center of your meditation. You will discover that it involves every part of yourself because the question, Who is the Lord to whom I pray? leads directly to the question, Who am I who wants to pray to the Lord? And then you will soon wonder, Why is the Lord of justice also the Lord of love; the God of fear also the God of gentle compassion? This leads you to the center of meditation.

Is there an answer? Yes and no. You will find out in your meditation. You might some day have a flash of understanding even while the question still remains and pulls you closer to God. But it is not a question that can be simply one of your questions. In a way, it needs to be your only question around which all that you do finds its place. It requires a certain decision to make that question the center of your meditation. If you do so, you will realize that you are embarking on a long road, a very long road."

— *The Genesee Diary*

On a Pilgrimage

Praying means, above all, to be accepting toward God who is always new, always different. For God is a deeply moved God whose heart is greater than ours. The open acceptance of prayer in the face of an ever-new God makes us free. In prayer, we are constantly on the way, on a pilgrimage. On our way, we meet more and more people who show us something about the God whom we seek. We will never know for sure if we have reached God. But we do know that God will always be new and that there is no reason to fear.

— *With Open Hands*

Anticipating Life in the Divine Kingdom

Prayer is the act by which we divest ourselves of all false belongings and become free to belong to God and God alone. This explains why, although we often feel a real desire to pray, we experience at the same time a strong resistance. We want to move closer to God, the source and goal of our existence, but at the same time we realize that the closer we come to God the stronger will be God's demand to let go of the many "safe" structures we have built around ourselves. Prayer is such a radical act because it requires us to criticize our whole way of being in the world, to lay down our old selves and accept our new self, which is Christ.

This is what Paul has in mind when he calls us to die with Christ so that we can live with Christ. It is to this experience of death and rebirth that Paul witnesses when he writes: "I live now not with my own life, but with the life of Christ who lives in me" (Gal. 2:20)....

In the act of prayer, we undermine the illusion of control by divesting ourselves of all false belongings and by directing ourselves totally to the God who is the only one to whom we belong. Prayer therefore is the act of dying to all that we consider to be our own and of being born to a new existence which is not of this world. Prayer is indeed a death to the world so that we can live for God. The great mystery of prayer is that even now it leads us into a new heaven and a new earth and thus is an anticipation of life in the divine kingdom. God is timeless, immortal, eternal, and prayer lifts us up into this divine life. — "Letting Go of All Things"

Prayer and Hope

To pray means to open your hands before God. It means slowly relaxing the tension which squeezes your hands to-gether and accepting your existence with an increasing readiness, not as a possession to defend, but as a gift to receive. Above all, prayer is a way of life which allows you to find a stillness in the midst of the world where you open your hands to God's promises and find hope for yourself, your neighbor, and your world. In prayer, you encounter God not only in the small voice and the soft breeze, but also in the midst of the turmoil of the world, in the distress and joy of your neighbor, and in the loneliness of your own heart.

— *With Open Hands*

Praying Is Living

Prayer leads you to see new paths and to hear new melodies in the air. Prayer is the breath of your life which gives you freedom to go and to stay where you wish and to find the many signs which point out the way to a new land. Praying is not simply some necessary compartment in the daily sched-ule of a Christian or a source of support in time of need, nor is it restricted to Sunday mornings or mealtimes. Praying is living. It is eating and drinking, action and rest, teaching and learning, playing and working. Praying pervades every aspect of our lives. It is the unceasing recognition that God is wherever we are, always inviting us to come closer and to celebrate the divine gift of being alive.   — *With Open Hands*

Three

Solitude

Solitude begins with a time and place for God, and God alone. — *Making All Things New*

In solitude we encounter not only God but also our true self. — *Clowning in Rome*

That Secret, Lonely Place

Without solitude it is virtually impossible to live a spiritual
life. Solitude begins with a time and place for God, and God
alone. If we really believe that God not only exists but also
is actively present in our lives — healing, teaching, and guiding — we need to set aside a time and space to give God
our undivided attention. Jesus says, "Go to your private room
and, when you have shut your door, pray to your Father who
is in that secret place" (Matt. 6:6).   — *Making All Things New*

To live a Christian life means to live *in* the world without
being *of* it. It is in solitude that this inner freedom can grow.
Jesus went to a lonely place to pray, that is, to grow in the
awareness that all the power he had was given to him; that
all the words he spoke came from his Father; and that all the
works he did were not really his but the works of the One
who had sent him. In the lonely place Jesus was made free
to fail.

A life without a lonely place, that is, a life without a quiet
center, easily becomes destructive. When we cling to the re-
sults of our actions as our only way of self-identification, then
we become possessive and defensive and tend to look at our
fellow human beings more as enemies to be kept at a distance
than as friends with whom we share the gifts of life.

In solitude we can slowly unmask the illusion of our pos-
sessiveness and discover in the center of our own self that
we are not what we can conquer, but what is given to us.
In solitude we can listen to the voice of the One who spoke
to us before we could speak a word, who healed us before
we could make any gesture to help, who set us free long before we could free others, and who loved us long before we

could give love to anyone. It is in this solitude that we discover that being is more important than having, and that we are worth more than the result of our efforts. In solitude we discover that our life is not a possession to be defended, but a gift to be shared. It's there we recognize that the healing words we speak are not just our own, but are given to us; that the love we can express is part of a greater love; and that the new life we bring forth is not a property to cling to, but a gift to be received. — *Out of Solitude*

Converting Loneliness into Solitude

In discussing [solitude and the need for it], three words are important: aloneness, loneliness, and solitude. You and I and all people are alone. Aloneness is a natural fact. No one else in the world is like me: I am unique. No one else feels and experiences the world the way I do: I am alone.

Now, how do I deal with my aloneness? Many people deal with it through loneliness. That means you experience your aloneness as a wound, as something that hurts you, makes you miserable. It makes you cry out, "Is there anyone who can help me?" Loneliness is one of the greatest sources of suffering today. It is the disease of our time.

But, as Christians, we are called to convert our loneliness into solitude. We are called to experience our aloneness not as a wound but as a gift — as God's gift — so that in our aloneness we might discover how deeply we are loved by God.

It is precisely where we are most alone, most unique, most ourselves, that God is closest to us. That is where we experience God as the divine, loving Father, who knows us better than we know ourselves.

Solitude is the way in which we grow into the realization that where we are most alone, we are most loved by God. It is a quality of heart, an inner quality that helps us to accept our aloneness lovingly, as a gift from God.

In that place our activities become activities done for the other. If we accept our aloneness as a gift from God, and convert it into deep solitude, then out of that solitude we can reach out to other people. We can come together in community, because we don't cling to one another out of loneliness. We don't use or manipulate one another. Rather, we bow to one another's solitude. We recognize one another as people who are called by the same God.

If I find God in my solitude, and you find God in your solitude, then the same God calls us together, and we can become friends. We can form a community, we can sustain a marriage, we can be together without destroying each other by clinging to each other.   — "A Quality of Heart"

Loneliness: A Precious Gift

But the more I think about loneliness, the more I think that the wound of loneliness is like the Grand Canyon — a deep incision in the surface of our existence which has become an inexhaustible source of beauty and self-understanding.

Therefore I would like to voice loudly and clearly what might seem unpopular and maybe even disturbing: The Christian way of life does not take away our loneliness; it protects and cherishes it as a precious gift. Sometimes it seems as if we do everything possible to avoid the painful confrontation with our basic human loneliness and allow ourselves to be trapped by false gods promising immediate satisfaction and quick relief. But perhaps the painful awareness of loneliness is an invitation to transcend our limitations and look beyond the boundaries of our existence. The awareness of loneliness might be a gift we must protect and guard, because our lone- liness reveals to us an inner emptiness that can be destructive when misunderstood, but filled with promise for the one who can tolerate its sweet pain.   — *The Wounded Healer*

The Discipline of Solitude

To bring some solitude into our lives is one of the most nec- essary but also most difficult disciplines. Even though we may have a deep desire for real solitude, we also experience a certain apprehension as we approach that solitary place and time. As soon as we are alone, without people to talk with, books to read, TV to watch, or phone calls to make, an inner chaos opens up in us. This chaos can be so disturbing and so confusing that we can hardly wait to get busy again. Entering a private room and shutting the door, therefore, does not mean that we immediately shut out all our inner doubts, anxieties, fears, bad memories, unresolved conflicts, angry feelings, and impulsive desires. On the contrary, when we have removed our outer distractions, we often find that our inner distractions manifest themselves to us in full force....

Solitude is not a spontaneous response to an occupied and preoccupied life. There are too many reasons not to be alone. Therefore we must begin by carefully planning some solitude. Five or ten minutes a day may be all we can tolerate. Per- haps we are ready for an hour every day, an afternoon every

week, a day every month, or a week every year. The amount
of time will vary for each person according to temperament,
age, job, lifestyle, and maturity. But we do not take the spiritual life seriously if we do not set aside some time to be
with and listen to God. We may have to write it in black
and white in our daily calendar so that nobody else can take
away this period of time. Then we will be able to say to our
friends, neighbors, students, customers, clients, or patients,
"I'm sorry, but I've already made an appointment at that time
and it can't be changed."

Once we have committed ourselves to spending time in
solitude, we develop an attentiveness to God's voice in us. In
the beginning, during the first days, weeks, or even months,
we may have the feeling that we are simply wasting our time.
Time in solitude may at first seem little more than a time
in which we are bombarded by thousands of thoughts and
feelings that emerge from hidden areas of our mind.

One of the early Christian writers describes the first stage
of solitary prayer as the experience of a man who, after years
of living with open doors, suddenly decides to shut them.
The visitors who used to come and enter his home start
pounding on his doors, wondering why they are not allowed
to enter. Only when they realize that they are not welcome
do they gradually stop coming. . . .

Intuitively, we know that it is important to spend time in
solitude. We even start looking forward to this strange period of uselessness. This desire for solitude is often the first
sign of prayer, the first indication that the presence of God's
Spirit no longer remains unnoticed. As we empty ourselves of
our many worries, we come to know not only with our mind
but also with our heart that we never were really alone, that
God's Spirit was with us all along. . . .

In solitude, we come to know the Spirit who has already been given to us. The pains and struggles we encounter in our solitude thus become the way to hope, because our hope is not based on something that will happen after our sufferings are over, but on the real presence of God's healing Spirit in the midst of these sufferings. The discipline of solitude allows us gradually to come in touch with this hopeful presence of God in our lives, and allows us also to taste even now the beginnings of the joy and peace which belong to the new heaven and the new earth. —*Making All Things New*

Confronting Our Nothingness

In order to understand the meaning of solitude, we must first unmask the ways in which the idea of solitude has been distorted by our world. We say to each other that we need some solitude in our lives. What we really are thinking of, however, is a time and place for ourselves in which we are not bothered by other people, can think our own thoughts, express our own complaints, and do our own thing, whatever it may be. For us, solitude most often means privacy. . . . We also think of solitude as a station where we can recharge our batteries, or as the corner of the boxing ring where our wounds are oiled, our muscles massaged, and our courage restored by fitting slogans. In short, we think of solitude as a place where we gather new strength to continue the ongoing competition in life.

But that is not the solitude of St. John the Baptist, of St. Anthony or St. Benedict, of Charles de Foucauld or the brothers of Taizé. For them solitude is not a private therapeutic place. Rather, it is the place of conversion, the place where

the old self dies and the new self is born, the place where the
emergence of the new man and the new woman occurs.

How can we gain a clearer understanding of this trans-
forming solitude? . . . In solitude I get rid of my scaffolding: no
friends to talk with, no telephone calls to make, no meetings
to attend, no music to entertain, no books to distract, just
me — naked, vulnerable, weak, sinful, deprived, broken —
nothing. It is this nothingness that I have to face in my solitude, a nothingness so dreadful that everything in me wants
to run to my friends, my work, and my distractions so that I
can forget my nothingness and make myself believe that I am
worth something. But that is not all. As soon as I decide to
stay in my solitude, confusing ideas, disturbing images, wild
fantasies, and weird associations jump about in my mind like
monkeys in a banana tree. Anger and greed begin to show
their ugly faces. . . . Thus I try again to run from the dark abyss
of my nothingness and restore my false self in all its vainglory.

The task is to persevere in my solitude, to stay in my
cell until all my seductive visitors get tired of pounding on
my door and leave me alone. . . . The wisdom of the desert is
that the confrontation with our own frightening nothingness
forces us to surrender ourselves totally and unconditionally
to the Lord Jesus Christ. Alone, we cannot face "the mystery of iniquity" with impunity. Only Christ can overcome
the powers of evil. Only in and through him can we survive
the trials of our solitude.   — *The Way of the Heart*

Allowing Something Creative to Happen

Silence means rest, rest of body and mind, in which we become available for God. This is very threatening. It is like

giving up control over our actions and thoughts, allowing something creative to happen not by us but to us. Is it so amazing that we are so often tired and exhausted, trying to be masters of ourselves, wanting to grasp the ultimate meaning of our existence, struggling with our identity? Silence is that moment in which we not only stop the discussion with others but also the inner discussions with ourselves, in which we can breathe freely and accept our identity as a gift. "Not I live, but He lives in me." It is in this silence that the Spirit of God can pray in us and continue its creative work in us.... Without silence the Spirit will die in us and the creative energy of our life will float away and leave us alone, cold and tired. Without silence we will lose our center and become victims of the many who constantly demand our attention.   —"Training for the Campus Ministry"

Silence and Voices of Light

Silence is the discipline that helps us to go beyond the entertainment quality of our lives. There we can let our sorrows and joys emerge from their hidden place and look us in the face, saying: "Don't be afraid; you can look at your own journey, its dark and light sides, and discover your way to freedom." We may find silence in nature, in our own houses, in a church or meditation hall. But wherever we find it, we should cherish it. Because it is in silence that we can truly acknowledge who we are and gradually claim ourselves as a gift from God.

At first silence might only frighten us. In silence we start hearing the voices of darkness: our jealousy and anger, our resentment and desire for revenge, our lust and greed, and our pain over losses, abuses, and rejections. These voices are often noisy and boisterous. They may even deafen us. Our most spontaneous reaction is to run away from them and return to our entertainment.

But if we have the discipline to stay put and not let these dark voices intimidate us, they will gradually lose their strength and recede into the background, creating space for the softer, gentler voices of the light.

These voices speak of peace, kindness, gentleness, goodness, joy, hope, forgiveness, and, most of all, love. They might at first seem small and insignificant, and we may have a hard time trusting them. However, they are very persistent and they will grow stronger if we keep listening. They come from a very deep place and from very far. They have been speaking to us since before we were born, and they reveal to us that there is no darkness in the One who sent us into the world, only light.   —*Can You Drink the Cup?*

A Solitude of the Heart

Although the discipline of solitude asks us to set aside time and space, what finally matters is that our hearts become like quiet cells where God can dwell, wherever we go and whatever we do. The more we train ourselves to spend time with God and God alone, the more we will discover that God is with us at all times and in all places. Then we will be able to recognize God even in the midst of a busy and active life. Once the solitude of time and space has become a solitude of the heart, we will never have to leave that solitude. We will be able to live the spiritual life in any place and any time. Thus the discipline of solitude enables us to live active lives

in the world, while remaining always in the presence of the
living God. — *Making All Things New*

Tending Our Inner Garden

To be calm and quiet by yourself is not the same as sleeping. In fact, it means being fully awake and following with
close attention every move going on inside you. It requires
the discipline to recognize the urge to get up and go again as
a temptation to look elsewhere for what is close at hand. It
offers the freedom to stroll in your own inner yard and rake
up the leaves and clear the paths so you can easily find the
way to your heart. Perhaps there will be fear and uncertainty
when you first come upon this "unfamiliar terrain," but slowly
and surely you will discover an order and a familiarity which
deepens your longing to stay at home.

With this new confidence, we recapture our own life
afresh, from within. Along with the new knowledge of our
"inner space" where feelings of love and hate, tenderness and
pain, forgiveness and greed are separated, strengthened, or
reformed, there emerges the mastery of the gentle hand. This
is the hand of the gardener who carefully makes space for a
new plant to grow and who doesn't pull weeds too rashly, but
uproots only those which threaten to choke the young life.

— *With Open Hands*

Encountering Our True Self

In solitude...fear and anger can slowly be unmasked as
manifestations of a false self, and in solitude they can lose

their power in the embrace of God's love. That is what St. John means when he says: "In love there can be no fear, but fear is driven out by perfect love" (1 John 4:18). In solitude we can gradually be led to the truth that we are who God made us to be. Therefore, solitude is a place of conversion. There we are converted from people who want to show each other what we have and what we can do into people who raise our open and empty hands to God in the recognition that all we are is a free gift from God. Thus, in solitude we encounter not only God but also our true self. In fact, it is precisely in the light of God's presence that we can see who we really are.   —*Clowning in Rome*

Fashioning Our Own Desert

We enter into solitude first of all to meet our Lord and to be with God and God alone. Our primary task in solitude, therefore, is not to pay undue attention to the many faces which assail us, but to keep the eyes of our mind and heart on the One who is our divine savior. Only in the context of grace can we face our sin; only in the place of healing do we dare to show our wounds; only with a single-minded attention to Christ can we give up our clinging fears and face our own true nature. As we come to realize that it is not we who live, but Christ who lives in us, that he is our true self, we can slowly let our compulsions melt away and begin to experience the freedom of the children of God. And then we can look back with a smile and realize that we aren't even angry or greedy any more.

What does all of this mean for us in our daily life? Even when we are not called to the monastic life, or do not have the physical constitution to survive the rigors of the desert, we are still responsible for our own solitude. Precisely because our secular milieu offers us so few spiritual disciplines, we have to develop our own. We have, indeed, to fashion our own desert where we can withdraw every day, shake off our compulsions, and dwell in the gentle healing presence of our Lord. — *The Way of the Heart*

A Compassionate Solidarity

It is in solitude that compassionate solidarity grows. In solitude we realize that nothing human is alien to us, that the roots of all conflict, war, injustice, cruelty, hatred, jealousy, and envy are deeply anchored in our own heart. In solitude our heart of stone can be turned into a heart of flesh, a rebellious heart into a contrite heart, and a closed heart into a heart that can open itself to all suffering people in a gesture of solidarity.

If you would ask the desert fathers why solitude gives birth to compassion, they would say, "Because it makes us die to our neighbor." At first this answer seems quite disturbing to a modern mind. But when we give it a closer look we can see that in order to be of service to others we have to die to them; that is, we have to give up measuring our meaning and value with the yardstick of others. To die to our neighbors means to stop judging them, to stop evaluating them, and thus to become free to be compassionate. Compassion can never coexist with judgment because judgment creates the distance, the distinction, which prevents us from really being with the other. — *The Way of the Heart*

Solitude and Community

Solitude is not a private space over against the public space of community, nor is it merely a healing space in which we restore ourselves for community life. Solitude and community belong together; each requires the other as do the center and circumference of a circle. Solitude without community leads us to loneliness and despair, but community without solitude hurls us into a "void of words and feelings" (Bonhoeffer)....

Solitude is essential to community life because in solitude we grow closer to each other. When we pray alone, study, read, write, or simply spend quiet time away from the places where we interact with each other directly, we are in fact participating fully in the growth of community. It is a fallacy to think that we grow closer to each other only when we talk, play, or work together. Much growth certainly occurs in such human interactions, but at least as much growth can take place when we enter into solitude. We take the other with us into solitude, and there the relationship grows and deepens. In solitude we discover each other in a way which physical presence makes difficult, if not impossible.

•

Solitude is inseparable from community because in solitude we affirm the deepest reality of our lives together, namely, that as a community we are like hands pointing to God in prayer. We might even say that community life itself is first of all a prayerful gesture. People do not form community when they cling to each other in order to survive the storms of the world, but they *do* form community when together they erect a living prayer in the midst of our anxiety-ridden human family.

All this suggests that life in solitude is a life in faith. By leaving behind from time to time our many self-affirming actions and becoming "useless" in the presence of God, we transcend our inner fears and apprehensions and affirm our God as the one in whose love we find our strength and security. — "Solitude and Community"

Four

The Holy Spirit

Prayer is not what is done by us, but rather what is done by the Holy Spirit in us. — Compassion

When we speak about the Holy Spirit, we speak about the breath of God breathing in us.

— Bread for the Journey

Life in the Spirit

Spiritual life is life in the Spirit or, more accurately, the life of the Spirit in us. It is this spiritual life that enables us to live with a new mind in a new time. Once we have understood this, the meaning of prayer becomes clear. It is the expression of the life of the Holy Spirit in us. Prayer is not what is done by us, but rather what is done by the Holy Spirit in us. To the Corinthians Paul writes, "No one can say, 'Jesus is Lord' unless he is under the influence of the Holy Spirit" (1 Cor. 12:3), and to the Romans he says, "The Spirit...comes to help us in our weakness. For when we cannot choose words in order to pray properly, the Spirit expresses our plea in a way that could never be put into words, and God who knows everything in our hearts knows perfectly well what he means, and that the pleas of the saints expressed by the Spirit are according to the mind of God" (Rom. 8:26–27). Prayer is the work of the Holy Spirit. — *Compassion*

God's Covenant

God made a covenant with us. The word "covenant" means "coming together." God wants to come together with us. In many of the stories in the Hebrew Bible, we see that God appears as a God who defends us against our enemies, protects us against dangers, and guides us to freedom. God is *God-for-us*. When Jesus comes a new dimension of the covenant is revealed. In Jesus, God is born, grows to maturity, lives, suffers, and dies as we do. God is *God-with-us*. Finally, when Jesus leaves he promises the Holy Spirit. In the Holy Spirit, God reveals the full depth of the covenant. God wants to be as close to us as our breath. God wants to breathe in us, so that all we say, think, and do is completely inspired by God. God is *God-within-us.* Thus, God's covenant reveals to us how much God loves us.   —*Bread for the Journey*

The Breath of God within Us

When we speak about the Holy Spirit, we speak about the breath of God breathing in us. The Greek word for "spirit" is *pneuma,* which means "breath." We are seldom aware of our breathing. It is so essential for life that we only think about it when something is wrong with it.

The Spirit of God is like our breath. God's Spirit is more intimate to us than we are to ourselves. We might not often be aware of it, but without it we cannot live a "spiritual life." It is the Holy Spirit of God who prays in us, who offers us the gifts of love, forgiveness, kindness, goodness, gentleness, peace, and joy. It is the Holy Spirit who offers us the life that death cannot destroy.   —*Bread for the Journey*

Perhaps the challenge of the Gospel lies precisely in the invitation to accept a gift for which we can give nothing in return. For the gift is the life breath of God, the Spirit poured out on us through Jesus Christ. This life breath frees us from fear and gives us new room to live. Those who live prayerfully are constantly ready to receive the breath of God and to let their lives be renewed and expanded. Those who never pray, on the contrary, are like children with asthma: because they are short of breath, the whole world shrivels up before them. They creep into a corner gasping for air and are vir-

tually in agony. But those who pray open themselves to God
and can breathe freely again.   — *With Open Hands*

Empowered to Call God "Abba"

Calling God "Abba, Father" is different from giving God a
familiar name. Calling God "Abba" is entering into the same
intimate, fearless, trusting, and empowering relationship with
God that Jesus had. This relationship is called Spirit, and this
Spirit is given to us by Jesus and enables us to cry out with
him, "Abba, Father."

Calling God "Abba, Father" (see Rom. 8:15; Gal. 4:6) is
a cry of the heart, a prayer welling up from our innermost
beings. It has nothing to do with naming God but everything
to do with claiming God as the source of who we are. This
claim does not come from any sudden insight or acquired
conviction; it is the claim that the Spirit of Jesus makes in
communion with our spirits. It is the claim of love.

                              — *Bread for the Journey*

A Window on Our Spiritual Lives

Even though our emotional and spiritual lives are distinct,
they do influence one another profoundly. Our feelings often
give us a window on our spiritual journeys. When we cannot
let go of jealousy, we may wonder if we are in touch with the
Spirit in us that cries out "Abba." When we feel very peaceful
and "centered," we may come to realize that this is a sign of
our deep awareness of our belovedness.

Likewise our prayer lives, lived as faithful response to the presence of the Spirit within us, may open a window on our emotions, feelings, and passions and give us some indication of how to put them in the service of our long journey into the heart of God.   — *Bread for the Journey*

At Home in God

The depth of our belonging to God is revealed by Jesus. His relation with God through the Holy Spirit is one of total openness. Everything Jesus owns is a gift from the Father. He never claims anything as just his apart from God. He says that we are called to enter the same relationship with the Father that he has, doing all that he does. In sending us the Holy Spirit, he says that we will be led into a full, intimate relationship with God, so that we won't have to be victims of the world's spirit.

Spiritually we are *in* God, *in* the Lord, *at home* in God. Our true identity is that we are God's children. It is from that perspective — from God's perspective — that we perceive the world. We are called to see the world as God sees it; that is what theology is all about. Therefore, we are continually diagnosing the illusory quality of anything outside this perspective.   — *The Road to Peace*

A Space That Can Contain All

Now I know that it is not I who pray but the Spirit of God who prays in me. Indeed, when God's glory dwells in me, there is nothing too far away, nothing too painful, nothing too strange or too familiar that it cannot contain and renew by its touch. Every time I recognize the glory of God in me and give it space to manifest itself to me, all that is human can be brought there and nothing will be the same again. Once in a while I just know it: Of course, God hears my prayer. God prays in me and touches the whole world with love right here and now. At those moments all questions about "the social relevance of prayer, etc." seem dull and very unintelligent, and the silent prayer of the monks one of the few things that keeps some sanity in this world.

—*The Genesee Diary*

An All-Embracing Intimacy

Many people tend to associate prayer with separation from others, but real prayer brings us closer to our fellow human beings. Prayer is the first and indispensable discipline of compassion precisely because prayer is also the first expression of human solidarity. Why is this so? Because the Spirit who prays in us is the Spirit by whom all human beings are brought together in unity and community. The Holy Spirit, the Spirit of peace, unity, and reconciliation, constantly reveals itself to us as the power through whom people from the most diverse social, political, economic, racial, and ethnic backgrounds are brought together as sisters and brothers of the same Christ and daughters and sons of the same Father.

To prevent ourselves from slipping into spiritual romanticism or pious sentimentality, we must pay careful attention to the compassionate presence of the Holy Spirit. The intimacy of prayer is the intimacy created by the Holy Spirit who, as the bearer of the new mind and the new time, does not exclude but rather includes our fellow human beings. In the intimacy of prayer, God is revealed to us as the One who loves all the members of the human family just as personally and uniquely as God loves us. Therefore, a growing intimacy with God deepens our sense of responsibility for others. It evokes in us an always increasing desire to bring the whole world with all its suffering and pains around the divine fire in our heart and to share the revitalizing heat with all who want to come.   —*Compassion*

Spiritual Rebirth

How can we describe the spiritual rebirth of which Jesus speaks to Nicodemus? An adequate description is impossible, precisely because this rebirth is beyond our intellectual and emotional grasp....

As to what spiritual rebirth is, however, we can say that persons reborn in the Spirit are characterized by their single-mindedness. They have only one desire: to do God's will in all things, or — to put it in Jesus' words to Nicodemus — to "do the truth" and thus to "come out into the light so that what they are doing may plainly appear as done in God" (John 3:21). They are so caught up in God's love that everything else can only receive its meaning and purpose in the context of that love. They ask only one question: "What is pleasing to the Spirit of God?" And as soon as they have heard the sound of the Spirit, they follow its promptings even when it upsets their friends, disturbs their environment, and confuses their admirers. They believe unhesitatingly in Jesus, the Son of God, who was sent into the world "not to judge the world, but so that through him the world might be saved" (John 3:17). Their faith is so deeply rooted that they are unafraid — not only of other people's opinions, but even of God's judgments, because their rebirth has brought them into the light....

At the same time, the spiritually reborn always call people together into community because the Spirit of God gathers all believers into one body. And the communities formed by the Spirit are not refuges designed to protect the interests of their members or to keep them at a safe distance from the world. They are holy places where everyone is intensely present first of all to the "very person of God, or more exactly to the three Divine Persons: to the Holy Spirit and through the Holy Spirit to Jesus and the Father."[1]

— "Reborn from Above"

Nurturing the Faith Within

Can we do something to be reborn from above, or is it all so dependent on the initiative of God's Spirit that we have no choice but to wait until it happens to us? The answer from all the Gospels is that an active faith in Jesus and the One who sent him is essential in receiving the Holy Spirit. Even though our rebirth is a completely free gift of the Holy Spirit, nevertheless we are ourselves fully a part of this rebirth.... Faith is the active trust in God who has promised us the Holy Spirit from above.

---

1. Thomas Philippe, "Fidelity to the Spirit," a pamphlet at La Ferme, a L'Arche foyer in Trosly-Bruil, France, p. 9.

Is there a way for us to nurture that faith within? The answer is yes: it is the way of poverty, the way that Jesus himself shows us as he moves toward the cross. Jesus consistently refuses the way of success, power, influence, and celebrity. Always, he chooses the way of weakness, powerlessness, compassion, and obscurity — the way of the poor. . . .

And so every time we choose poverty over wealth, powerlessness over power, humble service over popularity, quiet fruitfulness over loud acclaim, we prepare for our rebirth in the Holy Spirit. This might sound gloomy, unnatural, and even impossible. But once we have embarked on the journey of faith, our eyes will be opened to the way of the poor without any coercion or force. We will discover, first of all, our own poverty, fears, doubts, vulnerabilities, and weaknesses. In faith, we will no longer ignore or avoid these things, but embrace them as the place where Jesus walks with us and sends us his Spirit. Then also we will see clearly the poor around us, whether they are materially, emotionally, or mentally poor, and we will realize that they reveal to us God's presence, in ways nobody else could. We will feel drawn to them, not because of their poverty, but because of the Holy Spirit shining through their poverty.

Thus, the Spirit living in our poverty will speak to the Spirit among the poor. Our poor hearts will speak to the poor hearts of those around us. And out of this, a new spiritual community will be molded, not something spectacular, imposing, or world-convincing, but, on the contrary, something small, hidden, and very humble, scarcely noticed by our fast-moving world. In the midst of the world, but hidden from its view, something very new, very tender, and very fragile can be born. When such a new birth takes place in and among us, we will recognize it, even though we lack the words to express it fully. It is the work of the Holy Spirit, the Spirit from above. It is the greatest gift a human being can receive; a gift to be gently held, carefully protected, and patiently led to full maturity.   —"Reborn from Above"

Five

Belovedness

Prayer, then, is listening to that voice — to the One who calls you the Beloved.   — "Parting Words"

Prayer means entering into communion with the One who loved us before we could love. It is this "first love" (1 John 4:19) that is revealed to us in prayer.   — The Road to Peace

"You Are My Beloved"

I very much believe that the core moment of Jesus' public life was the baptism in the Jordan, when Jesus heard the affirmation, "You are my beloved on whom my favor rests." That is the core experience of Jesus. He is reminded in a deep, deep way of who he is. The temptations in the desert are temptations to move him away from that spiritual identity. He was tempted to believe he was someone else: *You are the one who can turn stone into bread. You are the one who can jump from the temple. You are the one who can make others bow to your power.* Jesus said, "No, no, no. I am the Beloved from God." I think his whole life is continually claiming that identity in the midst of everything. There are times in which he is praised, times when he is despised or rejected, but he keeps saying, *Others will leave me alone, but my Father will not leave me alone. I am the beloved Son of God. I am the hope found in that identity.*

Prayer, then, is listening to that voice — to the One who calls you the Beloved. It is to constantly go back to the truth of who we are and claim it for ourselves. I'm not what I do. I'm not what people say about me. I'm not what I have. Although there is nothing wrong with success, there is nothing wrong with popularity, there is nothing wrong with being powerful, finally my spiritual identity is not rooted in the world, the things the world gives me. My life is rooted in my spiritual identity. Whatever we do, we have to go back regularly to that place of core identity.   — "Parting Words"

God's Unconditional Love

What can we say about God's love? We can say that God's love is unconditional. God does not say, "I love you, if...." There are no "ifs" in God's heart. God's love for us does not depend on what we do or say, on our looks or intelligence, on our success or popularity. God's love for us existed before we were born and will exist after we have died. God's love is from eternity to eternity and is not bound to any time-related events or circumstances. Does that mean that God does not care what we do or say? No, because God's love wouldn't be real if God didn't care. To love without condition does not mean to love without concern. God desires to enter into relationship with us and wants us to love God in return.

— Bread for the Journey

We often confuse unconditional love with unconditional approval. God loves us without conditions but does not approve of every human behavior. God doesn't approve of betrayal, violence, hatred, suspicion, and all other expressions of evil, because they all contradict the love God wants to instill in the human heart. Evil is the absence of God's love. Evil does not belong to God.

God's unconditional love means that God continues to love us even when we say or think evil things. God continues to wait for us as a loving parent waits for the return of a lost child. It is important for us to hold on to the truth that God never gives up loving us even when God is saddened by what we do. That truth will help us to return to God's ever-present love.   *— Bread for the Journey*

Being in God's Love

To say with all that we have, think, feel, and are, "God exists" is the most world-shattering statement that a human being can make.... Because when God exists, all that *is* flows from God.... However, as soon as I say "God exists," my existence no longer can remain in the center, because the essence of the knowledge of God reveals my own existence as deriving its total being from God's. That is the true conversion experience. I no longer let the knowledge of my existence be the center from which I derive, project, deduct, or intuit the existence of God; I suddenly or slowly find my own existence revealed to me in and through the knowledge of God. Then it becomes real for me that I can love myself and my neighbor only because God has loved me first.

The life-converting experience is not the discovery that I have choices to make that determine the way I live out my existence but the answer that my existence itself is not in the center. Once I "know" God, that is, once I experience God's love as the love in which all my human experiences are anchored, I can only desire one thing: to be in that love. "Being" anywhere else, then, is shown to be illusory and eventually lethal. — *¡Gracias!*

Held Safe in Jesus' Love

As you see more clearly that your vocation is to be a witness to God's love in this world, and as you become more determined to live out that vocation, the attacks of the enemy will increase. You will hear voices saying, "You are worthless, you having nothing to offer, you are unattractive, undesirable, unlovable." The more you sense God's call, the more you will discover in your own soul the cosmic battle between God and Satan. Do not be afraid. Keep deepening your conviction that God's love for you is enough, that you are in safe hands, and that you are being guided every step of the way. Don't be surprised by the demonic attacks. They will increase, but as you face them without fear, you will discover that they are powerless....

The love of Jesus will give you an ever-clearer vision of your call as well as of the many attempts to pull you away from that call. The more you are called to speak for God's love, the more you will need to deepen the knowledge of that love in your own heart. The farther the outward journey takes you, the deeper the inward journey must be. Only when your roots are deep can your fruits be abundant. The enemy is there, waiting to destroy you, but you can face the enemy without fear when you know that you are held safe in the love of Jesus.

— *The Inner Voice of Love*

Knowing God and Knowing Ourselves

The mystery of the spiritual life is that Jesus desires to meet us in the seclusion of our own heart, to make his love known to us there, to free us from our fears, and to make our own deepest self known to us. In the privacy of our heart, therefore, we can learn not only to know Jesus, but through Jesus to know ourselves as well. If you reflect on this a bit more you will see an interaction between God's love revealing itself to you and a constant growth in self-knowledge. Each time you let the love of God penetrate deeper into your heart, you lose a bit of your anxiety; and every time you shed a bit of your anxiety, you learn to know yourself better and long all the more to be known by your loving God.

Thus the more you learn to love God, the more you learn to know and to cherish yourself. Self-knowledge and self-love are the fruit of knowing and loving God. You can see better now what is intended by the great commandment to "love the Lord your God with all your heart, with all your soul, and with all your mind, and to love your neighbor as yourself." Laying our hearts totally open to God leads to a love of ourselves that enables us to give whole-hearted love to our fellow human beings. In the seclusion of our hearts we learn to know the hidden presence of God; and with that spiritual knowledge we can lead a loving life.

— *Letters to Marc about Jesus*

Experiencing the First Love

Prayer means entering into communion with the One who loved us before we could love. It is this "first love" (1 John 4:19) that is revealed to us in prayer. The more deeply we enter into the house of God, the house whose language is prayer, the less dependent we are on the blame or praise of those who surround us, and the freer we are to let our whole being be filled with that first love. As long as we are still wondering what other people say or think about us and trying to act in ways that will elicit a positive response, we are still victimized and imprisoned by the dark world in which we live. In that dark world we have to let our surroundings tell us what we are worth. . . . As long as we are in the clutches of that world, we live in darkness, since we do not know our true self. We cling to our false self in the hope that maybe more success, more praise, more satisfaction will give us the experience of being loved, which we crave. That is the fertile ground of bitterness, greed, violence, and war.

In prayer, however, again and again we discover that the love we are looking for has already been given to us and that we can come to the experience of that love. Prayer is entering into communion with the One who molded our being in our mother's womb with love and only love. There, in the first love, lies our true self, a self not made up of the rejections and acceptances of those with whom we live, but solidly rooted in the One who called us into existence. In the house of God we were created. To that house we are called to return. Prayer is the act of returning.

— The Road to Peace

Returning to the First Love

For three days I have been meditating on the story of the prodigal son. It is a story about returning. I realize the importance of returning over and over again. My life drifts away from God. I have to return. My heart moves away from my first love. I have to return. My mind wanders to strange images. I have to return. Returning is a lifelong struggle.

It strikes me that the wayward son had rather selfish motivations. He said to himself, "How many of my father's paid servants have more food than they want, and here am I dying of hunger! I will leave this place and go to my father." He didn't return because of a renewed love for his father. No, he returned simply to survive. He had discovered that the way he had chosen was leading him to death. Returning to his father was a necessity for staying alive. He realized that he had sinned, but this realization came about because sin had brought him close to death.

I am moved by the fact that the father didn't require any higher motivation. His love was so total and unconditional that he simply welcomed his son home.

This is a very encouraging thought. God does not require a pure heart before embracing us. Even if we return only because following our desires has failed to bring happiness, God will take us back. Even if we return because being a Christian brings us more peace than being a pagan, God will receive us. Even if we return because our sins did not offer as much satisfaction as we had hoped, God will take us back. Even if we return because we could not make it on our own, God will receive us. God's love does not require any explanations about why we are returning. God is glad to see us home and wants to give us all we desire, just for being home.

—*The Road to Daybreak*

A Jealous Love

To return to God means to return to God with all that I am and all that I have. I cannot return to God with just half of my being. As I reflected this morning again on the story of the prodigal son and tried to experience myself in the embrace of the father, I suddenly felt a certain resistance to being embraced so fully and totally. I experienced not only a desire to be embraced, but also a fear of losing my independence. I realized that God's love is a jealous love. God wants not just a part of me, but all of me. Only when I surrender myself completely to God's parental love can I expect to be free from endless distractions, ready to hear the voice of love, and able to recognize my own unique call.

It is going to be a very long road. Every time I pray, I feel the struggle. It is the struggle of letting God be the God of my whole being. It is the struggle to trust that true freedom lies hidden in total surrender to God's love.

Following Jesus is the way to enter into the struggle and find true freedom. The way is the way of the cross, and true freedom is the freedom found in the victory over death. Jesus' total obedience to his Father led him to the cross, and through the cross to a life no longer subject to the competitive games of this world. Jesus held on to nothing, not even to satisfying religious experiences. His words "My God, my God, why have you forsaken me?" give us a glimpse of the complete surrender of Jesus to his Father. Nothing was left for him to cling to. In this complete surrender he found total unity and total freedom.

To me Jesus says, "Come and follow me...I have come so that you may have life and have it abundantly" (John 10:10).

— The Road to Daybreak

Living under the Blessing

The great spiritual call of the Beloved Children of God is to pull their brokenness away from the shadow of the curse and put it under the light of the blessing. This is not as easy as it sounds. The powers of the darkness around us are strong, and our world finds it easier to manipulate self-rejecting people than self-accepting people. But when we keep listening attentively to the voice calling us the Beloved, it becomes possible to live our brokenness, not as a confirmation of our fear that we are worthless, but as an opportunity to purify and deepen the blessing that rests upon us.

Physical, mental, or emotional pain lived under the blessing is experienced in ways radically different from physical, mental, or emotional pain lived under the curse. Even a small burden, perceived as a sign of our worthlessness, can lead us to deep depression — even suicide. However, great and heavy burdens become light and easy when they are lived in the light of the blessing. What seemed intolerable becomes a challenge. What seemed a reason for depression becomes a source of purification. What seemed punishment becomes a gentle pruning. What seemed rejection becomes a way to a deeper communion.   —*Life of the Beloved*

Moving into the House of Love

Jesus speaks to us in the Gospel with very strong words. Throughout the Gospel, we hear, "Do not be afraid." That is what Gabriel says to Zechariah. That is what Gabriel says to Mary. That is what the angels say to the women at the tomb: "Do not be afraid." And that is what the Lord...says when he appears to his disciples: "Do not be afraid, it is I. *Do not be afraid, it is I.* Fear is not of God. I am the God of love, a God who invites you to receive — to receive the gifts of joy and peace and gratitude of the poor, and to let go of your fears so that you can start sharing what you are so afraid to let go of."

The invitation of Christ is the invitation to move out of the house of fear and into the house of love: to move away out of that place of imprisonment into a place of freedom. "Come to me, come to my house which is the house of love,"

Jesus says. Throughout the Old and the New Testaments we see that invitation: "Oh, how much I desire to dwell in the house of the Lord. The Lord is my refuge, the Lord is my dwelling place, the Lord is my tent, the Lord is my safety." "Where do you live?" the disciples ask. "Come and see," the Lord says. And they stayed with him. The Word became flesh and pitched its tent among us so that God could dwell among us in the house of love. "And I am going to the Father to prepare a house for you, a space for you, because in the dwelling place of my Father there are many places for you. Make your home in me as I have made my home in you. Live in the name of the Lord — the name of the place where you should dwell. Where are you? Are you in the name? Are you in the place of love?"

— *The Road to Peace*

Responding to God's Love

God says, "I love you with an everlasting love," and Jesus came to tell us that. When Jesus was baptized, he heard a voice that said, "You are my beloved, on whom God's favor rests." That's a very important statement that Jesus wants us to hear. We are the Beloved, not because we did anything, not because we proved ourselves. Basically, God loves us whatever we do. If that's true, these few years that we are in the world, we are sent to say, in the midst of our life, "Yes, God, I love you, too."

Just as God cares for us, it's very important that we care for God in the world. If God is born like a little baby, God cannot walk or speak unless someone teaches God. That's the story of Jesus, who needs human beings in order to grow. God is saying, "I want to be weak so you can love me. What better way to help you respond to my love than becoming weak so you can care for me?" God becomes a stumbling God who falls at the cross, who dies for us, and who is totally in need of love. God does this so that we can get close. The God who loves us is a God who becomes vulnerable, dependent in the manger and dependent on the cross, a God who basically is saying, "Are you there for me?"

God, you could say, is waiting for our answer. In a very mysterious way, God is dependent on us. God is saying, "I want to be vulnerable, I need your love. I have a desire for your affirmation of my love." God is a jealous God in the sense of wanting our love and wanting us to say yes. That's why in the end of the Gospel of John, Jesus asks Peter three times, "Do you love me?" God is waiting for us to respond. Life gives us endless opportunities for that response.

—*The Road to Peace*

Jesus could walk faithfully through life. He was praised and he was criticized, he was admired and he was despised; he was asked to be king and he was crucified. But he was faithful to the Voice. That is what prayer is all about....

Jesus went at night to pray, to listen to the Voice, to claim he is already the Beloved. Immediately after that, he heard another voice. The devil said: "You have to prove you are the Beloved. Change stone to bread or jump from the temple and the angels will catch you — get some power and have influence." Jesus said: "I don't have to prove I am the Beloved; I am already."

For us to work for justice and peace and really be activists in the good sense of the word is to do it not because we need to prove to ourselves or anybody that we are worth loving. Rather, it is because we are so in touch with our belovedness that we are free to act according to the truth and say no to injustice and say yes when we see justice and peace.

I feel that once we are in touch with our belovedness, we will better see the gifts that come to us from people who affirm that in us. Therefore, the great obstacle which prevents the Spirit working in us is self-rejection. The greatest obstacle to the Spirit working in us is that we say to ourselves that we are useless, we are nothing.

Once I know I am the Beloved, once I start discovering that in me, then the Spirit can work in me and in others; then we can do wonderful things. Now, once I say, "No, God doesn't love me, I am not as good as everyone else," somehow I do not claim the truth that Jesus came to proclaim.

— "Discipleship and Reconciliation"

The First and Second Commandments

Jesus' primary concern was to be obedient to his Father, to live constantly in his presence. Only then did it become clear to him what his task was in his relationships with people. This also is the way he proposes for his apostles: "It is to the glory of my Father that you should bear much fruit, and then you will be my disciples" (John 15:8). Perhaps we must continually remind ourselves that the first commandment requiring us to love God with all our heart, all our soul, and all our mind is indeed the first. I wonder if we really believe this. It seems that in fact we live as if we should give as much of our heart, soul, and mind as possible to our fellow human beings, while trying hard not to forget God. At least we feel that our attention should be divided evenly between God and our neighbor.

But Jesus' claim is much more radical. He asks for a single-minded commitment to God and God alone. God wants all of our heart, all of our mind, and all of our soul. It is this unconditional and unreserved love for God that leads to the care for our neighbor, not as an activity which distracts us from God or competes with our attention to God, but as an expression of our love for God who is revealed to us as the God of all people. It is in God that we find our neighbors and discover our responsibility to them. We might even say that only in God does our neighbor become a neighbor rather than an infringement upon our autonomy, and that only in and through God does service become possible.

— The Living Reminder

Prayer is not merely a condition for compassionate leadership: it is its essence. As long as we keep speaking about prayer as a way to restore ourselves from spiritual fatigue, or worse, to recharge our batteries, we have reduced prayer to a method and compassion to a commodity. Reminding each other that we should not forget to pray in our busy lives is like reminding each other to keep breathing! Prayer is the essence of the spiritual life without which all ministry loses its meaning. It is the fulfillment of the great commandment to love the Lord our God with all our heart, all our soul, and all our mind. Our heart, soul, and mind can never be divided between God and neighbor. God is a jealous God who wants our love without any reservations. But in our total, undivided commitment to God, God is revealed to us as the God of our neighbor and so makes our love for God a love that embraces all people in time and place. Therefore, the second commandment is like the first. Therefore, union with God is solidarity with all humanity. Therefore, all real mystics are reformers of people, and prayer is the mother and father, brother and sister of all compassion.

— "Compassion: The Core of Spiritual Leadership"

Offering Blessings

The characteristic of the blessed ones is that, wherever they go, they always speak words of blessing. It is remarkable how easy it is to bless others, to speak good things to and about them, to call forth their beauty and truth, when you yourself are in touch with your own blessedness. The blessed one always blesses. And people want to be blessed! This is so apparent wherever you go. No one is brought to life through curses, gossip, accusations, or blaming. There is so much of that taking place around us all the time. And it calls forth only darkness, destruction, and death. As the "blessed ones," we can walk through this world and offer blessings. It doesn't require much effort. It flows naturally from our hearts. When we hear within ourselves the voice calling us by name and blessing us, the darkness no longer distracts us. The voice that calls us the Beloved will give us words to bless others and reveal to them that they are no less blessed than we.

— *Life of the Beloved*

Six

Listening

The core of all prayer is indeed listening.

—Making All Things New

Praying is first and foremost listening to Jesus, who dwells in the very depths of your heart.

—Letters to Marc about Jesus

Being All Ear for God

It is clear that we are usually surrounded by so much inner
and outer noise that it is hard to truly hear our God when
God is speaking to us. We have often become deaf, unable to
know when God calls us and unable to understand in which
direction God calls us. Thus our lives have become absurd.
In the word "absurd" we find the Latin word *surdus,* which
means "deaf."

A spiritual life requires discipline because we need to learn
to listen to God, who constantly speaks but whom we seldom
hear. When, however, we learn to listen, our lives become
obedient lives. The word "obedient" comes from the Latin
word *audire,* which means "listening." A spiritual discipline
is necessary in order to move slowly from an absurd to an
obedient life, from a life filled with noisy worries to a life
in which there is some free inner space where we can listen
to our God and follow God's guidance. Jesus' life was a life
of obedience. He was always listening to the Father, always
attentive to his voice, always alert for his directions. Jesus
was "all ear." That is true prayer: being all ear for God. The
core of all prayer is indeed listening, obediently standing in
the presence of God.   —*Making All Things New*

Attentive Listening

When we enter into solitude we will often hear these two
voices — the voice of the world and the voice of the Lord —
pulling us in two contrary directions. But if we keep returning faithfully to the place of solitude, the voice of the
Lord will gradually become stronger and we will come to

know and understand with mind and heart the peace we are searching for.

What do we do in our solitude? The first answer is nothing. Just be present to the One who wants your attention and listen! It is precisely in this "useless" presence to God that we can gradually die to our illusions of power and control and give ear to the voice of love hidden in the center of our being. But "doing nothing, being useless," is not as passive as it sounds. In fact it requires effort and great attentiveness. It calls us to an active listening in which we make ourselves available to God's healing presence and can be made new.

— *The Road to Peace*

A Listening Heart

The discipline of the heart . . . makes us aware that praying is not only listening *to* but also listening *with*. The discipline of the heart makes us stand in the presence of God with all we have and are: our fears and anxieties, our guilt and shame, our sexual fantasies, our greed and anger, our joys, successes, aspirations and hopes, our reflections, dreams and mental wandering, and most of all our people, family, friends and enemies, in short, all that makes us who we are. With all this we have to listen to God's voice and allow God to speak to us in every corner of our being. This is very hard since we are so fearful and insecure that we keep hiding ourselves from God.

We tend to present to God only those parts of ourselves with which we feel relatively comfortable and which we think will evoke a positive response. Thus our prayer becomes very selective and narrow. And not just our prayer but also our

self-knowledge, because by behaving as strangers before God
we become strangers to ourselves.   — "Spiritual Direction"

The Still Small Voice

Why is it so difficult to be still and quiet and let God speak
to me about the meaning of my life? Is it because I don't trust
God? Is it because I don't know God? Is it because I wonder
if God really is there for me? Is it because I am afraid of God?
Is it because everything else is more real for me than God? Is
it because, deep down, I do not believe that God cares what
happens at the corner of Yonge and Bloor?

Still there is a voice — right there, in downtown Toronto.
"Come to me, you who labor and are overburdened, and I
will give you rest. Shoulder my yoke and learn from me, for
I am gentle and humble in heart, and you will find rest for
your soul. Yes, my yoke is easy and my burden light" (Matt.
11:28–30).

Can I trust that voice and follow it? It is not a very loud
voice, and often it is drowned out by the clamor of the
inner city. Still, when I listen attentively, I will hear that
voice again and again and come to recognize it as the voice
speaking to the deepest places of my heart.   — *Here and Now*

Listening to the Blessing

For me personally, prayer becomes more and more a way to
listen to the blessing. I have read and written much about
prayer, but when I go to a quiet place to pray, I realize that,
although I have a tendency to say many things to God, the

real "work" of prayer is to become silent and listen to the voice that says good things about me. This might sound self-indulgent, but, in practice, it is a hard discipline. I am so afraid of being cursed, of hearing that I am no good or not good enough, that I quickly give in to the temptation to start talking and to keep talking in order to control my fears. To gently push aside and silence the many voices that question my goodness and to trust that I will hear a voice of blessing . . . that demands real effort.

Have you ever tried to spend a whole hour doing nothing but listening to the voice that dwells deep in your heart? . . . It is not easy to enter into the silence and reach beyond the many boisterous and demanding voices of our world and to discover there the small intimate voice saying: "You are my Beloved Child, on you my favor rests." Still, if we dare to embrace our solitude and befriend our silence, we will come to know that voice. I do not want to suggest to you that one day you will hear that voice with your bodily ears. I am not speaking about a hallucinatory voice, but about a voice that can be heard by the ear of faith, the ear of the inner heart.

— Life of the Beloved

A New Beginning

We must learn to live each day, each hour, yes, each minute as a new beginning, as a unique opportunity to make everything new. Imagine that we could live each moment as a moment pregnant with new life. Imagine that we could live each day as a day full of promises. Imagine that we could walk through the new year always listening to a voice saying

to us: "I have a gift for you and can't wait for you to see it!"
Imagine.

Is it possible that our imagination can lead us to the truth
of our lives? Yes, it can! The problem is that we allow our
past, which becomes longer and longer each year, to say to
us: "You know it all; you have seen it all, be realistic; the
future will be just another repeat of the past. Try to survive
it as best you can." There are many cunning foxes jumping
on our shoulders and whispering in our ears the great lie:
"There is nothing new under the sun . . . don't let yourself be
fooled. . . ."

So what are we to do? First, we must send the foxes back
to where they belong: in their foxholes. And then we must
open our minds and our hearts to the voice that resounds
through the valleys and hills of our life saying: "Let me show
you where I live among my people. My name is 'God-with-
you.' I will wipe away all the tears from your eyes; there will
be no more death, and no more mourning or sadness. The
world of the past has gone" (see Rev. 21:2–5).

We must choose to listen to that voice, and every choice
will open us a little more to discover the new life hidden in
the moment, waiting eagerly to be born.   — *Here and Now*

Listening with a Sacred Text

It might be helpful to offer here a concrete suggestion. One
good way to listen is to listen with a sacred text: a psalm
or a prayer, for instance. The Hindu spiritual writer Eknath
Easwaran showed me the great value of learning a sacred text
by heart and repeating it slowly in the mind, word by word,
sentence by sentence. In this way, listening to the voice of

love becomes not just a passive waiting, but an active attentiveness to the voice that speaks to us through the words of
the Scriptures.

I spent many of my half-hours of prayer doing nothing but
slowly repeating the prayer of St. Francis: "Lord make me an
instrument of your peace. Where there is hatred let me sow
love...." As I let these words move from my mind to my
heart, I began to experience, beyond all my restless emotions
and feelings, the peace and love I was asking for in words.

In this way I also had a way to deal with my endless distractions. When I found myself wandering away far and wide,
I could always return to my simple prayer and thereby listen
again in my heart to the voice I so much wanted to hear.

—Life of the Beloved

Three Forms of Listening

How can we keep listening to this voice in a world which
does its best to distract us and get our attention for seemingly
more urgent matters?...I want to put before you...three
forms of listening that for me have proven to be the most
productive.

First of all, listen to the church.... I'm deeply convinced
that the greatest spiritual danger for our times is the separation of Jesus from the church. The church is the body of
the Lord. Without Jesus there can be no church; and without
the church we cannot stay united with Jesus. I've yet to meet
anyone who has come closer to Jesus by forsaking the church.
To listen to the church is to listen to the Lord of the church.
Specifically, this entails taking part in the church's liturgical
life. Advent, Christmas, Lent, Easter, Ascension, and Pente-

cost: these seasons and feasts teach you to know Jesus better and better and unite you more and more intimately with the divine life he offers you in the church.

The Eucharist is the heart of the church's life. It's there that you hear the life-giving Gospel and receive the gifts that sustain that life within you. The best assurance that you'll go on listening to the church is your regular participation in the Eucharist.

Second, listen to the book. By that I mean read the Bible; read books about the Bible, about the spiritual life, and the lives of "great" saints. . . . Many people are brought to God through spiritual literature that they chance or choose to read. Augustine, Ignatius, Thomas Merton, and many others have been converted through the book. The challenge, however, is not to read a "spiritual" book as a source of interesting information, but rather to listen to it as to a voice that addresses you directly. It isn't easy to let a text "read" you. Your thirst for knowledge and information often makes you desire to own the word, instead of letting the word own you. Even so, you will learn the most by listening carefully to the Word that seeks admission to your heart.

Finally, listen to your heart. It's there that Jesus speaks most intimately to you. Praying is first and foremost listening to Jesus, who dwells in the very depths of your heart. He doesn't shout. He doesn't thrust himself upon you. His voice is an unassuming voice, very nearly a whisper, the voice of a gentle love. Whatever you do with your life, go on listening to the voice of Jesus in your heart. This listening must be an active and very attentive listening, for in our restless and noisy world Jesus' loving voice is easily drowned out. You need to set aside some time every day for this active listening to Jesus, if only for ten minutes. Ten minutes each day for Jesus alone can bring about a radical change in your life.

—*Letters to Marc about Jesus*

Listening Together

In our wordy world we usually spend our time together talking. We feel most comfortable in sharing experiences, discussing interesting subjects, or arguing about current issues. It is through a very active verbal exchange that we try to discover each other. But often we find that words function more as walls than as gates, more as ways to keep distance than to come close. Often — even against our own desires — we find ourselves competing with each other. We try to prove to each other that we are worth being paid attention to, that we have something to show that makes us special.

The discipline of community helps us to be silent together. This disciplined silence is not an embarrassing silence, but a silence in which together we pay attention to the Lord who calls us together. In this way we come to know each other not as people who cling anxiously to our self-constructed identity, but as people who are loved by the same God in a very intimate and unique way. . . .

It is often the words of Scripture that can lead us into this communal silence. Faith, as Paul says, comes from hearing. We have to hear the word from each other. When we come together from different geographical, historical, psychological, and religious directions, listening to the same word spoken by different people can create in us a common openness and vulnerability that allow us to recognize that we are safe together in that word. Thus we can come to dis-cover our true identity as a community, thus we can come to experience what it means to be called together, and thus we can recognize that the same Lord whom we discovered in our solitude also speaks in the solitude of our neighbors, whatever their language, denomination, or character.

In this listening together to the word of God, a true cre-ative silence can grow. This silence is a silence filled with the caring presence of God. Thus listening together to the word can free us from our competition and rivalry and allow us to recognize our true identity as sons and daughters of the same loving God and brothers and sisters of our Lord Jesus Christ, and thus of each other.   —*Making All Things New*

Seven

Discipline

A spiritual life without discipline is impossible.

—Making All Things New

Discipline means that something very specific and concrete needs to be done to create the context in which a life of uninterrupted prayer can develop.

—Clowning in Rome

Setting Our Hearts on the Kingdom

How... can we move from fragmentation to unity, from many
things to the one necessary thing, from our divided lives to
undivided lives in the Spirit? A hard struggle is required. It
is the struggle to allow God's Spirit to work in us and re-
create us. But this struggle is not beyond our strength. It calls
for some very specific, well-planned steps. It calls for a few
moments a day in the presence of God when we can listen
to God's voice precisely in the midst of our many concerns.
It also calls for the persistent endeavor to be with others in
a new way by seeing them not as people to whom we can
cling in fear, but as fellow human beings with whom we can
create new space for God. These well-planned steps, these
disciplines, are the concrete ways of "setting your hearts on
the kingdom," and they can slowly dismantle the power of
our worries and thus lead us to unceasing prayer.

The beginning of the spiritual life is often difficult not only
because the powers which cause us to worry are so strong
but also because the presence of God's Spirit seems barely
noticeable. If, however, we are faithful to our disciplines, a
new hunger will make itself known. This new hunger is the
first sign of God's presence. When we remain attentive to
this divine presence, we will be led always deeper into the
kingdom.   — *Making All Things New*

With Open Hands

In a society that seems to be filled with urgencies and emer-
gencies, prayer appears to be an unnatural form of behavior.

Without fully realizing it, we have accepted the idea that "doing things" is more important than prayer and have come to think of prayer as something for times when there is nothing urgent to do....

Concentrated human effort is necessary because prayer is not our most natural response to the world. Left to our own impulses, we will always want to do something else before we pray. Often, what we want to do seems so unquestionably good — setting up a religious education program, helping with a soup kitchen, listening to people's problems, visiting the sick, planning the liturgy, working with prisoners or mental patients — that it is hard to realize that even these things can be done with impatience and so become signs of our own needs rather than of God's compassion.

Therefore, prayer is in many ways the criterion of Christian life. Prayer requires that we stand in God's presence with open hands, naked and vulnerable, proclaiming to ourselves and to others that without God we can do nothing. This is difficult in a climate where the predominant counsel is, "Do your best and God will do the rest." When life is divided into "our best" and "God's rest," we have turned prayer into a last resort to be used only when all our own resources are depleted. Then even the Lord has become the victim of our impatience. Discipleship does not mean to use God when we can no longer function ourselves. On the contrary, it means to recognize that we can do nothing at all, but that God can do everything through us. As disciples, we find not some but all of our strength, hope, courage, and confidence in God. Therefore, prayer must be our first concern. — *Compassion*

Creating Boundaries around Our Meeting with God

We simply need quiet time in the presence of God. Although we want to make all our time, time for God, we will never succeed if we do not reserve a minute, an hour, a morning, a day, a week, a month, or whatever period of time for God and God alone. This asks for much discipline and risk taking because we always seem to have something more urgent to do and "just sitting there" and "doing nothing" often disturbs us more than it helps. But there is no way around this. Being useless and silent in the presence of our God belongs to the core of all prayer. In the beginning we often hear our own unruly inner noises more loudly than God's voice. This is at times very hard to tolerate. But slowly, very slowly, we discover that the silent time makes us quiet and deepens our awareness of ourselves and God. Then, very soon, we start missing these moments when we are deprived of them, and before we are fully aware of it an inner momentum has developed that draws us more and more into silence and closer to that still point where God speaks to us.

Contemplative reading of the Holy Scriptures and silent time in the presence of God belong closely together. The word of God draws us into silence; silence makes us attentive to God's word. The word of God penetrates through the thick of human verbosity to the silent center of our heart; silence opens in us the space where the word can be heard. Without reading the word, silence becomes stale, and without silence, the word loses its recreative power. The word leads to silence and silence to the word. The word is born in silence, and silence is the deepest response to the word.

— *Reaching Out*

That is why prayer requires discipline. Discipline means to create boundaries around our meeting with God. Our times and places can't be so filled up that there is no way of meeting. So you have to work very hard to say this is the time in which I am with God, whether I like it or not, whether I feel like it, whether it satisfies me. It is very interesting that people who follow a prayer discipline for ten minutes a day or so, when they keep doing it regularly, eventually, they don't want to miss it — even though it doesn't satisfy right away on the level of the flesh. They may be distracted throughout the whole ten minutes, but they keep going back to it. They say, "Something is happening to me on a deeper level than my thinking. I don't have wonderful thoughts when I pray nor do I have wonderful feelings when I pray, but God is greater than my heart and my mind."

The larger mystery of prayer is greater than what I can grasp with my emotional senses or intellectual gifts. I trust that God is greater than me when I dwell — let myself be held — in that place of prayer. — "Parting Words"

Prayer-Practice

Without discipline, unceasing prayer remains a vague ideal, something that has a certain romantic appeal but that is not very realistic in our contemporary world. Discipline means that something very specific and concrete needs to be done to create the context in which a life of uninterrupted prayer can develop. Unceasing prayer requires the discipline of prayer exercises. Those who do not set aside a certain place and time each day to do nothing else but pray can never expect their unceasing thought to become unceasing prayer.

Why is this planned prayer-practice so important? It is important because through this practice God can become fully present to us as a real partner in our conversation. . . .

It is of primary importance that we strive for prayer with the understanding that it is an explicit way of being with God. We often say, "All of life should be lived in gratitude," but this is possible only if at certain times we give thanks in a very concrete and visible way. We often say, "All our days should be lived for the glory of God," but this is possible only if a day is regularly set apart to give glory to God. We often say, "We should love one another always," but this is possible only if we regularly perform concrete and unambiguous acts of love. Similarly, it is also true that we can say, "All our thoughts should be prayer," only if there are times in which we make God our only thought. . . .

Many people still have the impression that contemplative prayer is something very special, very "high," or very difficult, and really not for ordinary people with ordinary jobs and ordinary problems. This is unfortunate because the discipline of contemplative prayer is particularly valuable for those who have so much on their minds that they suffer from fragmentation. If it is true that all Christians are called to bring their thoughts into an ongoing conversation with their Lord, then contemplative prayer can be a discipline that is especially important for those who are deeply involved in the many affairs of this world.   *— Clowning in Rome*

Developing Patience

Prayer as a discipline of patience is the human effort to allow the Holy Spirit to do its re-creating work in us. . . . The discipline of prayer makes us stop and listen, wait and look, taste and see, pay attention and be aware. Although this may sound like advice to be passive, it actually demands much willpower and motivation. We may consider the discipline of prayer a form of inner displacement. The ordinary and proper response to our world is to turn on the radio, open the newspaper, go to another movie, talk to more people, or look impatiently for new attractions and distractions. To listen patiently to the voice of the Spirit in prayer is a radical displacement which at first creates unusual discomfort. We are so accustomed to our impatient way of life that we do not expect much from the moment. Every attempt to "live it through" or to "stay with it" is so contrary to our usual habits that all our impulses rise up in protest. But when discipline keeps us faithful, we slowly begin to sense that something so deep, so mysterious, and so creative is happening here and now that we are drawn toward it — not by our impulses but by the Holy Spirit. In our inner displacement, we experience the presence of the compassionate God.   — *Compassion*

Remaining Faithful: John Eudes's Answer

This morning I put this question to John Eudes: "How can I really develop a deep prayer life when I am back again at my busy work?" John Eudes's answer was clear and simple: "The only solution is a prayer schedule that you will never break without consulting your spiritual director. Set a time that is reasonable, and once it is set, stick to it at all costs. Make it your most important task. Let everyone know that this is the only thing you will not change and pray at that time.... When you remain faithful, you slowly discover that

it is useless to think about your many problems since they
won't be dealt with in that time anyhow. Then you start saying to yourself during these free hours, 'Since I have nothing
to do now, I might just as well pray!' So praying becomes
as important as eating and sleeping, and the time set free
for it becomes a very liberating time to which you become
attached in the good sense."   —*The Genesee Diary*

Mother Teresa's Answer

Once, quite a few years ago, I had the opportunity of meeting
Mother Teresa of Calcutta. I was struggling with many things
at the time and decided to use the occasion to ask Mother
Teresa's advice. As soon as we sat down I started explain-
ing all my problems and difficulties — trying to convince her
of how complicated it all was! When, after ten minutes of
elaborate explanation, I finally became silent, Mother Teresa
looked at me quietly and said: "Well, when you spend one
hour a day adoring your Lord and never do anything which
you know is wrong...you will be fine!"

When she said this, I realized, suddenly, that she had
punctured my big balloon of complex self-complaints and
pointed me far beyond myself to the place of real healing.
...Her few words became engraved on my heart and mind
and remain to this day. I had not expected these words, but
in their directness and simplicity, they cut through to the
center of my being. I knew that she had *spoken* the truth and
that I had the rest of my life to *live* it.   —*Here and Now*

Spiritual Reading

An important discipline in the life of the Spirit is spiritual reading. Through spiritual reading we have some say over what enters into our minds. Each day our society bombards us with a myriad of images and sounds. Driving down Yonge Street in downtown Toronto is like driving through a dictionary: each word demanding our attention in all sorts of sizes and colors and with all sorts of gestures and noises. The words yell and scream at us: "Eat me, drink me, buy me, hire me, look at me, talk with me, sleep with me!" Whether we ask for it or not is not the question; we simply cannot go far without being engulfed by words and images forcibly intruding themselves into our minds. But do we really want our mind to become the garbage can of the world? . . .

Clearly we do not, but it requires real discipline to let God and not the world be the Lord of our mind. But that asks of us not just to be gentle as doves, but also cunning as serpents! Therefore spiritual reading is such a helpful discipline. Is there a book we are presently reading, a book that we have selected because it nurtures our mind and brings us closer to God? Our thoughts and feelings would be deeply affected if we were always to carry with us a book that puts our minds again and again in the direction we want to go. . . . Even if we were to read for only fifteen minutes a day in such a book, we would soon find our mind becoming less of a garbage can and more of a vase filled with good thoughts.

— Here and Now

Bible Reading and Contemplation

To take the Holy Scriptures and read them is the first thing
we have to do to open ourselves to God's call. Reading the
Scriptures is not as easy as it seems since in our academic
world we tend to make anything and everything we read subject to analysis and discussion. But the word of God should
lead us first of all to contemplation and meditation. Instead
of taking the words apart, we should bring them together in
our innermost being; instead of wondering if we agree or dis-
agree, we should wonder which words are directly spoken to
us and connect directly with our most personal story. Instead
of thinking about the words as potential subjects for an interesting dialogue or paper, we should be willing to let them
penetrate into the most hidden corners of our heart, even to
those places where no other word has yet found entrance.
Then and only then can the word bear fruit as seed sown
in rich soil. Only then can we really "hear and understand"
(Matt. 13:23).   — *Reaching Out*

One very simple discipline for contemplative prayer is to
read, every evening before going to sleep, the readings of the
next day's Eucharist with special attention to the Gospel. It
is often helpful to take one sentence or word that offers special comfort and repeat it a few times so that, with that one
sentence or word, the whole content can be brought to mind
and allowed slowly to descend from the mind into the heart.

I have found this practice to be a powerful support in
times of crisis. It is especially helpful during the night, when
worries or anxieties may keep me awake and seduce me into
idolatry. By remembering the Gospel story or any of the say-
ings of the Old or New Testament authors, I can create a safe

mental home into which I can lead all my preoccupations and let them be transformed into quiet prayer.

During the following day, a certain time must be set apart for explicit contemplation. This is a time in which to look at Christ as he appears in the reading. The best way to do this is to read the Gospel of the day again and to imagine the Lord as he speaks or acts with his people. In this hour we can see him, hear him, touch him, and make him present to our whole being. We can see Christ as our healer, our teacher, and our guide. We can see him in his indignation, in his compassion, in his suffering, and in his glory. We can look at him, listen to him, and enter into conversation with him. . . .

For me, this discipline of having an "empty time" just to be with Christ as he speaks to me in the readings of the day has proven very powerful. I have discovered that during the rest of the day, wherever I am or whatever I am doing, the image of Christ that I have contemplated during that "empty time" stays with me as a beautiful icon. Sometimes it is the conscious center of all my thoughts, but more often it is a quiet presence of which I am only indirectly aware. . . .

This simple discipline of prayer can do much to provide a strong framework in which our unceasing thought can become unceasing prayer. In contemplative prayer, Christ cannot remain a stranger who lived long ago in a foreign world. Rather, he becomes a living presence with whom we can enter into dialogue here and now.   — *Clowning in Rome*

Compline is such an intimate and prayerful moment that some people in the neighborhood come daily to the Abbey to join in this most quiet prayer of the day. I start realizing that the psalms of Compline slowly become flesh in me;

they become part of my night and lead me to a peaceful sleep.... Trust is written all through the evening prayer:

> He who dwells in the shelter of the Most High
> and abides in the shade of the Almighty
> says to the Lord: "My refuge,
> my stronghold, my God in whom I trust!"
>
> It is he who will free you from the snare
> of the fowler who seeks to destroy you;
> he will conceal you with his pinions
> and under his wings you will find refuge. (Ps. 91)

Slowly these words enter into the center of my heart. They are more than ideas, images, comparisons: They become a real presence. After a day with much work or with many tensions, you feel that you can let go in safety and realize how good it is to dwell in the shelter of the Most High.

— The Genesee Diary

Knowing by Heart

One simple and somewhat obvious technique is memorization. The expression "to know by heart" already suggests its value. Personally I regret the fact that I know so few prayers and psalms by heart. Often I need a book to pray, and without one I tend to fall back on the poor spontaneous creations of my mind. Part of the reason, I think, that it is so hard to pray "without ceasing" is that few prayers are available to me outside church settings. Yet I believe that prayers which I know by heart could carry me through very painful crises. The Methodist minister Fred Morris told me how Psalm 23 ("The Lord is my shepherd") had carried him through the gruesome hours in the Brazilian torture chamber and had given him peace in his darkest hour. And I keep wondering which words I can take with me in the hour when I have to survive without books. I fear that in crisis situations I will have to depend on my own unredeemed ramblings and not have the word of God to guide me. — *The Living Reminder*

Spiritual Guidance

Word and silence both need guidance. How do we know that we are not deluding ourselves, that we are not selecting those words that best fit our passions, that we are not just listening to the voice of our own imagination? Many have quoted the Scriptures and many have heard voices and seen visions in silence, but only a few have found their way to God. Who can be the judge in his own case? Who can determine if her feelings and insights are leading her in the right direction? Our God is greater than our own heart and mind, and too easily we are tempted to make our heart's desires and our mind's speculations into the will of God. Therefore, we need a guide, a director, a counselor who helps us to distinguish between the voice of God and all the other voices coming from our own confusion or from dark powers far beyond our control. We need someone who encourages us when we are tempted to give it all up, to forget it all, to just walk away in despair. We need someone who discourages us when we move too rashly in unclear directions or hurry proudly to a nebulous goal. We need someone who can suggest to us when to read and when to be silent, which words to reflect upon and what to do when silence creates much fear and little peace.

— *Reaching Out*

It is of great value to submit our prayer life from time to time to the supervision of a spiritual guide. A spiritual director in this strict sense is not a counselor, a therapist, or an analyst, but a mature fellow Christian to whom we choose to be accountable for our spiritual life and from whom we can expect prayerful guidance in our constant struggle to discern God's active presence in our lives. A spiritual director can be called "soul-friend" (Kenneth Leech) or a "spiritual friend" (Tilden Edwards). It is important that he or she practices the disciplines of the Church and the Book and thus become familiar with the space in which we try to listen to God's voice.

The way we relate to our spiritual director depends very much on our needs, our personalities, and our external circumstances. Some people may want to see their spiritual director bi-weekly or monthly; others will find it sufficient to be in touch only when the occasion asks for it. Some people may feel the need for a more extensive sharing with their spiritual director, while others will find seeing him or her once in a while for a few short moments to be sufficient. It is essential that one Christian help another Christian to enter without fear into the presence of God and there to discern God's call.   — "Spiritual Direction"

Perhaps the 1970s offer us a unique chance to reclaim the rich tradition of schooling in prayer. All spiritual writers, from the desert fathers to Teresa of Avila, Evelyn Underhill, and Thomas Merton, have stressed the great power and central importance of prayer in our lives....

If this is true, then it is obvious that prayer requires supervision and direction. Just as verbatim reports of our conversations with patients can help us to deepen our interpersonal sensitivities, so a continuing evaluation of our spiritual life can lead us closer to God. If we do not hesitate to study how love and care reveal themselves in encounters between people, then why should we shy away from detailed attention to the relationship with the One who is the source and purpose of all human interactions?   — *The Living Reminder*

Disciplines for the Journey Home

Going home is a lifelong journey. There are always parts of ourselves that wander off in dissipation or get stuck in resentment. Before we know it we are lost in lustful fantasies or angry ruminations. Our night dreams and daydreams often remind us of our lostness.

Spiritual disciplines such as praying, fasting, and caring are ways to help us return home. As we walk home we often realize how long the way is. But let us not be discouraged. Jesus walks with us and speaks to us on the road. When we listen carefully we discover that we are already home while on the way.   — *Bread for the Journey*

Eight

Unceasing Prayer

The prayer has become the active presence of God's Spirit guiding me through life.

— *The Way of the Heart*

Prayer can become unceasing prayer when all our thoughts . . . can be thought in the presence of God.

— *Clowning in Rome*

Prayer as All of Life

When we think about prayer, we usually regard it as one of the many things we do to live a full and mature Christian life.... If we are fervent in our conviction that prayer is important, we might even be willing to give a whole hour to prayer every day, or a whole day every month, or a whole week every year. Thus prayer becomes a part, a very important part, of our life.

But when the apostle Paul speaks about prayer, he uses a very different language. He does not speak about prayer as a part of life, but as all of life. He does not mention prayer as something we should not forget, but claims it is our ongoing concern. He does not exhort his readers to pray once in a while, regularly, or often, but without hesitation admonishes them to pray constantly, unceasingly, without interruption. Paul does not ask us to spend some of every day in prayer. No, Paul is much more radical. He asks us to pray day and night, in joy and in sorrow, at work and at play, without intermissions or breaks. For Paul, praying is like breathing. It cannot be interrupted without mortal danger.

—Clowning in Rome

Fearless Conversation with God

To pray unceasingly, as St. Paul asks us to do, would be completely impossible if it meant to think constantly about God.... To pray, I think, does not mean to think about God in contrast to thinking about other things, or to spend time with God instead of spending time with other people. Rather, it means to think and live in the presence of God. As soon as we begin to divide our thoughts into thoughts about God and thoughts about people and events, we remove God from our daily life to a pious little niche where we can think pious thoughts and experience pious feelings.

Although it is important and even indispensable for the spiritual life to set apart time for God and God alone, prayer can only become unceasing prayer when all our thoughts — beautiful or ugly, high or low, proud or shameful, sorrowful or joyful — can be thought in the presence of God. Thus, converting our unceasing thinking into unceasing prayer moves us from a self-centered monologue to a God-centered dialogue. . . .

To pray unceasingly is to lead all our thoughts out of their fearful isolation into a fearless conversation with God. Jesus' life was a life lived in the presence of God his Father. Jesus kept nothing, absolutely nothing, hidden from his Father's face. Jesus' joys, his fears, his hopes, and his despairs were always shared with his Father.   — *Clowning in Rome*

Prayer is not introspection. It is not a scrupulous, inward-looking analysis of our own thoughts and feelings but a careful attentiveness to the One who invites us to an unceasing conversation. Prayer is the presentation of all thoughts — reflective thoughts as well as daydreams and night dreams — to our loving Father so that God can see them and respond to them with divine compassion. Prayer is the joyful affirmation that God knows our minds and hearts and that nothing is hidden from God. It is saying with Psalm 139 (Grail translation, Paulist Press):

> O Lord, you search me and you know me,
> you know my resting and my rising,
> you discern my purpose from afar.

You mark when I walk or lie down,
all my ways lie open to you. (vv. 1–3)

O search me, God, and know my heart.
O test me and know my thoughts.
See that I follow not the wrong path
and lead me in the path of life eternal. (vv. 23–24)

Prayer is a radical conversion of all our mental processes, because in prayer we move away from ourselves — our worries, preoccupations, and self-gratifications — and direct all that we recognize as ours to God in the simple trust that through God's love all will be made new.

But this conversion from unceasing thought to unceasing prayer is far from easy. There is a deep resistance to making ourselves so vulnerable, so naked, so totally unprotected. We indeed want to love God and worship God, but we also want to keep a little corner of our inner life for ourselves, where we can hide and think our own secret thoughts, dream our own dreams, and play with our own mental fabrications. We are always tempted to select carefully the thoughts that we bring into our conversations with God.

What makes us so stingy? Maybe we wonder if God can take all that goes on in our minds and hearts. Can God accept our hateful thoughts, our cruel fantasies, and our shameful dreams? Can God handle our primitive images, our inflated illusions, and our exotic mental castles? Or do we want to hold on to our own pleasurable imaginings and stimulating reveries, afraid that in showing them to our Lord we may have to give them up? Thus we are constantly tempted to fall back into introspection out of fear or out of greed, and to keep from our God what often is most in need of God's healing touch. — *Clowning in Rome*

A Useless Hour to Be with God

If we relate to the world just in terms of usefulness and what
we can do with it, then we might not relate to it in such a
way that God can speak through it. It is very important that
once in a while we have an hour to be useless. Prayer is not
being busy with God instead of being busy with other things.
Prayer is primarily a useless hour.... Prayer is primarily to do
nothing in the presence of God. It is to be not useful and so
to remind myself that if anything important in life happens,
it is God who does it. So when I go into the day, I go with
the conviction that God is the one who brings fruits to my
work, and I do not have to act as though I am in control of
things. I have to work hard; I have to do my task. And at
the end of the day I have to keep saying that if something
good happens, let us praise the Lord for it. But in order to do
that, we had better take some time out and experience being
present for God and God alone, and that is not so easy.

—"Prayer and Ministry"

The Way of Simple Prayer

One simple [way] to move from the mind to the heart [is]
by slowly saying a prayer with as much attentiveness as possible. This may sound like offering a crutch to someone who
asks you to heal his broken leg. The truth, however, is that
a prayer, prayed from the heart, heals. When you know the
Our Father, the Apostles' Creed, the "Glory Be to the Father" by heart, you have something to start with. You might
like to learn by heart the Twenty-third Psalm: "The Lord is
my shepherd ... " or Paul's words about love to the Corinthi-

ans or St. Francis's prayer: "Lord, make me an instrument of your peace...." As you lie in your bed, drive your car, wait for the bus, or walk your dog, you can slowly let the words of one of these prayers go through your mind simply trying to listen with your whole being to what they are saying. You will be constantly distracted by your worries, but if you keep going back to the words of the prayer, you will gradually dis- cover that your worries become less obsessive and that you really start to enjoy praying. And as the prayer descends from your mind into the center of your being you will discover its healing power. — *Here and Now*

You wonder what to do when you feel attacked on all sides by seemingly irresistible forces, waves that cover you and want to sweep you off your feet. Sometimes these waves consist of feeling rejected, feeling forgotten, feeling misunderstood. Sometimes they consist of anger, resentment, or even the de- sire for revenge, and sometimes of self-pity and self-rejection. These waves make you feel like a powerless child abandoned by your parents.

What are you to do? Make the conscious choice to move the attention of your anxious heart away from these waves and direct it to the One who walks on them and says, "It's me. Don't be afraid" (Matt. 14:27; Mark 6:50; John 6:20). Keep turning your eyes to him and go on trusting that he will bring peace to your heart. Look at him and say, "Lord, have mercy." Say it again and again, not anxiously but with confidence that he is very close to you and will put your soul to rest. — *The Inner Voice of Love*

An Imagining of Jesus

Contemplative prayer is prayer in which we attentively look at God. How is this possible, since nobody can see God and live? The mystery of the Incarnation is that it has become possible to see God in and through Jesus Christ. Christ is the image of God. In and through Christ, we know that God is a loving Father whom we can see by looking at his Son. . . . Contemplative prayer, therefore, means to see Christ as the image of God. . . . All the images consciously or unconsciously created by our minds should be made subject to Jesus, who is the only image of God. Contemplative prayer can be described as an imagining of Christ, a letting him enter fully into our consciousness so that he becomes the icon always present in our inner room. By looking at Christ with loving attention, we learn with our minds and hearts what it means that he is the way to the Father. Jesus is the only one who has seen the Father. Jesus says, "Not that anybody has seen the Father, except the one who comes from God" (John 6:46). Jesus' whole being is a perpetual seeing of the Father. Jesus' life and works are an uninterrupted contemplation of his Father. For us, therefore, contemplation means an always increasing imagining of Jesus so that in, through, and with him, we can see the Father and live in God's presence.   — *Clowning in Rome*

God's way can only be grasped in prayer. The more you listen to God speaking within you, the sooner you will hear that voice inviting you to follow the way of Jesus. For Jesus' way is God's way, and God's way is not for Jesus only, but for everyone who is truly seeking God. Here we come up against the hard truth that the descending way of Jesus is also the way for us to find God. Jesus doesn't hesitate for a moment to make that clear. Soon after he has ended his period of fasting in the wilderness and calls his first disciples to follow him, he says,

> How blessed are the poor in spirit...
> Blessed are the gentle...
> Blessed are those who mourn...
> Blessed are those who hunger and thirst for
>   uprightness...
> Blessed are the merciful...
> Blessed are the pure in heart...
> Blessed are the peacemakers...
> Blessed are those who are persecuted in the cause of
>   uprightness...

Jesus is drawing a self-portrait here and inviting his disciples to become like him. He will continue to speak in this way to the very end. Jesus never makes a distinction between himself and his followers. His sorrow will be theirs; his joy they too will taste. He says, "If they persecuted me, they will persecute you too; if they kept my word, they will keep yours as well." As he speaks, they too must speak; as he behaves, they too must behave; as he suffers, they too must suffer. In all things Jesus is their example, and even more than that: he is their model. —*Letters to Marc about Jesus*

The Way of Downward Mobility

Prayer means letting God's creative love touch the most hidden places of our being, and letting Jesus' way of the cross, his way of downward mobility, truly become our way. And prayer means listening with attentive, undivided hearts, to the inner movements of the Spirit of Jesus, even when that Spirit leads us to places we would rather not go. . . .

I say this with great compassion: we are living in an upwardly mobile society, a society in which making it to the top is expected in some degree of all of us. And aren't we tempted to use even the Word of God to help us in this upward mobility? But that is not the way of God, the Father, Son, and Spirit. God's way is not the way of upward mobility but of downward mobility. You know, as well as I do, that the question we will finally hear is not going to be: "How much did you earn during your lifetime?" or "How many friends did you make?" or "How much progress did you make in your career?" No, the question for us will be: "What did you do for the least of mine? What did you do for the lonely in your cities, the prisoners in your country, the refugees within and below your borders, and the hungry all over the world? Have you seen the humiliated Christ in the faces of the poor?"

God has chosen to be revealed in a crucified humanity. That is a very hard realization to come to, yet all authentic prayer will eventually lead us to it. I hope you are able to feel with me our hesitation to let God truly love us in God's way and to respond fully with our whole being.

— "Prayer and the Jealous God"

Opening the Eyes of Our Soul

The desert fathers . . . point us toward a very holistic view of prayer. They pull us away from our intellectualizing practices, in which God becomes one of the many problems we have to address. They show us that real prayer penetrates to the marrow of our soul and leaves nothing untouched. The prayer of the heart is a prayer that does not allow us to limit our relationship with God to interesting words or pious emotions. By its very nature such prayer transforms our whole being into Christ precisely because it opens the eyes of our soul to the truth of ourselves as well as to the truth of God. In our heart we come to see ourselves as sinners embraced by the mercy of God. It is this vision that makes us cry out, "Lord Jesus Christ, Son of the living God, have mercy on me, a sinner." The prayer of the heart challenges us to hide absolutely nothing from God and to surrender ourselves unconditionally to God's mercy.   — *The Way of the Heart*

The Jesus Prayer

The Jesus prayer consists of the simple words: "Lord Jesus Christ, have mercy upon me." ... There is probably no simpler nor livelier way to understand the richness of ... the Jesus prayer than by listening to the remarkable story of an anonymous Russian peasant who wandered through his vast country discovering with growing amazement and inner joy the marvelous fruits of the Jesus prayer. In *The Way of a Pilgrim* his story is written down, most probably by a Russian monk whom he met on his journey....

> *The Way of the Pilgrim* ... begins as follows: "By the grace of God I am a Christian man, but by my actions a great sinner. ... On the twenty-fourth Sunday after Pentecost I went to church to say my prayers there during the Liturgy. The first Epistle of St. Paul to the Thessalonians was being read, and among other words

I heard these — 'Pray without ceasing' [1 Thess. 5:17].
It was this text, more than any other, which forced itself upon my mind, and I began to think how it was
possible to pray without ceasing, since a man has to
concern himself with other things also in order to make
a living."[1]

The peasant went from church to church to listen to ser-
mons but did not find the answer he desired. Finally, he met
a holy *staretz*, who said to him: "Ceaseless interior prayer is a
continual yearning of the human spirit toward God. To succeed in this consoling exercise we must pray more often to
God to teach us to pray without ceasing. Pray more, and pray
more fervently. It is prayer itself which will reveal to you how
it can be achieved unceasingly; but it will take some time."[2]

Then the holy *staretz* taught the peasant the Jesus Prayer:
"Lord Jesus Christ, have mercy on me." While traveling as a
pilgrim through Russia, the peasant repeats this prayer thousands of times with his lips. He even considers the Jesus
Prayer to be his true companion. And then one day he has
the feeling that the prayer by its own action passes from his
lips to his heart. He says: "It seemed as though my heart in its
ordinary beating began to say the words of the Prayer within
at each beat....I gave up saying the Prayer with my lips. I
simply listened carefully to what my heart was saying."[3]

Here we learn of another way of arriving at unceasing
prayer. The prayer continues to pray within me even when
I am talking with others or concentrating on manual work.

---

1. R. M. French, trans., *The Way of the Pilgrim* (New York: Seabury Press,
1965), 1.
2. Ibid., 2–3.
3. Ibid., 19–20.

The prayer has become the active presence of God's Spirit guiding me through life.   —*Reaching Out; The Way of the Heart*

The Practice of the Presence of God

Unceasing prayer is not just the unusual feat of a simple Russian peasant, but a realistic vocation for all Christians. It certainly is not a way of living that comes either automatically by simply desiring it or easily by just praying once in a while. But when we give it serious attention and develop an appropriate discipline, we will see a real transformation in our lives that will lead us closer and closer to God. Unceasing prayer as a permanent and unchangeable state of mind obviously will never be reached. It will always require our attention and discipline. Nevertheless, we will discover that many of the disturbing thoughts that seemed to distract us are being transformed into the ongoing praise of God. When we see with increasing clarity the beauty of the Father through his Son, we will discover that created things no longer distract us. On the contrary, they will speak in many ways about him. Then we will realize that prayer is neither more nor less than the constant practice of the presence of God at all times and in all places.   —*Clowning in Rome*

The Prayer of the Heart

To stand in the presence of God with our mind in our heart, that is the essence of the prayer of the heart.... If prayer were just an intelligent exercise of our mind, we would soon become stranded in fruitless and trivial inner debates with God. If, on the other hand, prayer would involve only our heart, we might soon think that good prayers consist in good feelings. But the prayer of the heart in the most profound sense unites mind and heart in the intimacy of the divine love.

It is about this prayer that the pilgrim speaks, thereby expressing in his own charming naïve style the profound wisdom of the spiritual fathers of his time. In the expression "Lord Jesus Christ, have mercy upon me," we find a powerful summary of all prayer. It directs itself to Jesus, the Son of God, who lived, died, and was raised for us; it declares him to be the Christ, the anointed one, the Messiah, the one we have been waiting for; it calls him our Lord, the Lord of our whole being: body, mind, and spirit, thought, emotions, and actions; and it professes our deepest relationship to him by a confession of our sinfulness and by a humble plea for his forgiveness, mercy, compassion, love, and tenderness.[4]

The prayer of the heart can be a special guide to present-day Christians searching for our own personal way to an intimate relationship to God. More than ever we feel like wandering strangers in a fast-changing world. But we do not want to escape this world. Instead, we want to be fully part of it without drowning in its stormy waters. We want to be alert and receptive to all that happens around us without being paralyzed by inner fragmentation. We want to travel with open eyes through this valley of tears without losing contact with the One who calls us to a new land. We want to re-

---

4. See Anthony Bloom, *Living Prayer* (Springfield, Ill.: Templegate, 1966); *Beginning to Pray* (New York: Paulist Press, 1970); *Courage to Pray* (New York: Paulist Press, 1973).

spond with compassion to all those whom we meet on our way and ask for a hospitable place to stay while remaining solidly rooted in the intimate love of our God.

The prayer of the heart shows us one possible way. It is indeed like a murmuring stream that continues underneath the many waves of every day and opens the possibility of living in the world without being of it and of reaching out to our God from the center of our solitude. — *Reaching Out*

The Kingdom of God Is within You

The prayer of the heart requires first of all that we make God our only thought. That means that we must dispel all distractions, concerns, worries, and preoccupations and fill the mind with God alone. The Jesus prayer, or any other prayer form, is meant to be a help to gently empty our minds from all that is not God and offer all the room to God ... alone. But that is not all. Our prayer becomes a prayer of the heart when we have localized in the center of our inner being the empty space in which our God-filled mind can descend and vanish, and where the distinctions between thinking and feeling, knowing and experiencing, ideas and emotions are transcended, and where God can become our host.

"The Kingdom of God is within you," Jesus said (Luke 17:21). The prayer of the heart takes these words seriously. When we empty our mind from all thoughts and our heart from all experiences, we can prepare in the center of our innermost being the home for the God who wants to dwell in us. Then we can say with St. Paul, "I live now not with my own life but with the life of Christ who lives in me" (Gal. 2:20). Then we can affirm Luther's words, "Grace is the experience of being delivered from experience." And then we can realize that it is not we who pray, but the Spirit of God who prays in us.   — *Reaching Out*

Tabor and Gethsemane

Prayer ... is far from sweet and easy. Being the expression of our greatest love, it does not keep pain away from us. Instead, it makes us suffer more since our love for God is a love for a suffering God and our entering into God's intimacy is an entering into the intimacy where all of human suffering is embraced in divine compassion. To the degree that our prayer has become the prayer of our heart we will love more and suffer more, we will see more light and more darkness, more grace and more sin, more of God and more of humanity. To the degree that we have descended into our heart and reached out to God from there, solitude can speak to solitude, deep to deep, and heart to heart. It is there where love and pain are found together.

On two occasions, Jesus invited his closest friends, Peter, John, and James, to share in his most intimate prayer. The first time he took them to the top of Mount Tabor, and there they saw his face shining like the sun and his clothes white as light (Matt. 17:2). The second time he took them to the garden of Gethsemane, and there they saw his face in anguish and his sweat falling to the ground like great drops of blood (Luke 22:44). The prayer of our heart brings us both to Tabor and Gethsemane. When we have seen God in glory we will also see God in ... misery, and when we have felt the ugliness of God's humiliation we also will experience the beauty of the transfiguration.   — *Reaching Out*

A Heart That Embraces the Universe

The prayer of the heart ... includes all our concerns. When we enter with our mind into our heart and there stand in the presence of God, then all our mental preoccupations become prayer. The power of the prayer of the heart is precisely that through it all that is on our mind becomes prayer.

When we say to people, "I will pray for you," we make a very important commitment. The sad thing is that this remark often remains nothing but a well-meant expression of concern. But when we learn to descend with our mind into our heart, then all those who have become part of our lives are led into the healing presence of God and are touched by God in the center of our being. We are speaking here about a mystery for which words are inadequate. It is the mystery that the heart, which is the center of our being, is transformed ... into God's own heart, a heart large enough to embrace the entire universe. Through prayer we can carry in our heart all human pain and sorrow, all conflicts and agonies, all torture and war, all hunger, loneliness, and misery, not because of some great psychological or emotional capacity, but because God's heart has become one with ours.

— *The Way of the Heart*

Nine

Community

The community of faith is indeed the climate and source of all prayer. —Reaching Out

Many people tend to associate prayer with separation from others, but real prayer brings us closer to our fellow human beings. —Compassion

The Community of Faith

Just because prayer is so personal and arises from the center of our life, it is to be shared with others. Just because prayer is the most precious expression of being human, it needs the constant support and protection of the community to grow and flower. Just because prayer is our highest vocation needing careful attention and faithful perseverance, we cannot allow it to be a private affair. Just because prayer asks for a patient waiting in expectation, it should never become the most individualistic expression of the most individualistic emotion, but should always remain embedded in the life of the community of which we are part.

Prayer as a hopeful and joyful waiting for God is a really unhuman or superhuman task unless we realize that we do not have to wait alone. In the community of faith we can find the climate and the support to sustain and deepen our prayer, and we are enabled to constantly look forward beyond our immediate and often narrowing private needs. The community of faith offers the protective boundaries within which we can listen to our deepest longings, not to indulge in morbid introspection, but to find our God to whom they point. In the community of faith we can listen to our feelings of loneliness, to our desires for an embrace or a kiss, to our sexual urges, to our cravings for sympathy, compassion, or just a good word; also to our search for insight and to our hope for companionship and friendship. In the community of faith we can listen to all these longings and find the courage, not to avoid them or cover them up, but to confront them in order to discern God's presence in their midst. There we can affirm each other in our waiting and also in the realization that in the center of our waiting the first intimacy with God is found. There we can be patiently together and let the suffering of each day convert our illusions into the prayer of a contrite people. The community of faith is indeed the climate and source of all prayer. — *Reaching Out*

The Mosaic That Makes God Visible

Nothing is sweet or easy about community. Community is a fellowship of people who do not hide their joys and sorrows but make them visible to each other in a gesture of hope. In community we say: "Life is full of gains and losses, joys and sorrows, ups and downs — but we do not have to live it alone. We want to drink our cup together and thus celebrate the truth that the wounds of our individual lives, which seem intolerable when lived alone, become sources of healing when we live them as part of a fellowship of mutual care."

Community is like a large mosaic. Each little piece seems so insignificant. One piece is bright red, another cold blue or dull green, another warm purple, another sharp yellow, another shining gold. Some look precious, others ordinary. Some look valuable, others worthless. Some look gaudy, others delicate. As individual stones, we can do little with them except compare them and judge their beauty and value. When, however, all these little stones are brought together in one big mosaic portraying the face of Christ, who would ever question the importance of any one of them? If one of them, even the least spectacular one, is missing, the face is incomplete. Together in the one mosaic, each little stone is indispensable and makes a unique contribution to the glory of God. That's community, a fellowship of little people who together make God visible in the world. — *Can You Drink the Cup?*

The Call to Community

By ceasing to make our individual differences a basis of competition and by recognizing these differences as potential
contributions to a rich life together, we begin to hear the call
to community. In and through Christ, people of different ages
and lifestyles, from different races and classes, with different
languages and educations, can join together and witness to
God's compassionate presence in our world. There are many
common-interest groups, and most of them seem to exist in
order to defend or protect something. Although these groups
often fulfill important tasks in our society, the Christian community is of a different nature. When we form a Christian
community, we come together not because of similar experiences, knowledge, problems, color, or sex, but because we
have been called together by the same Lord. Only God enables us to cross the many bridges that separate us; only God
allows us to recognize each other as members of the same
human family; and only God frees us to pay careful attention
to each other. This is why those who are gathered together in
community are witnesses to the compassionate Lord. By the
way they are able to carry each other's burdens and share
each other's joys, they testify to God's presence in our world.
                                                    —*Compassion*

The Christian community is . . . a community which not only
creates a sense of belonging but also a sense of estrange-
ment. In the Christian community we say to each other,
"We are together, but we cannot fulfill each other . . . we
help each other, but we also have to remind each other
that our destiny is beyond our togetherness." The support
of the Christian community is a support in common expec-

tation. That requires a constant criticism of anyone who makes the community into a safe shelter or a cozy clique, and a constant encouragement to look forward to what is to come.

The basis of the Christian community is not the family tie, or social or economic equality, or shared oppression or complaint, or mutual attraction...but the divine call. The Christian community is not the result of human efforts. God has made us into chosen people by calling us out of "Egypt" to the "New Land," out of the desert to fertile ground, out of slavery to freedom, out of our sin to salvation, out of captivity to liberation. All these words and images give expression to the fact that the initiative belongs to God and that God is the source of our new life together. By our common call to the New Jerusalem, we recognize each other on the road as brothers and sisters. Therefore, as the people of God, we are called *ekklesia* (from the Greek *kaleo,* call; and *ek,* out), the community called out of the old world into the new.

— *Reaching Out*

Prayer as the Language of the Community

Prayer is the language of the Christian community.... By prayer, community is created as well as expressed. Prayer is first of all the realization of God's presence in the midst of God's people and, therefore, the realization of the community itself. Most clear and most noticeable are the words, the gestures, and the silence through which the community is formed. When we listen to the word, we not only receive insight into God's saving work, but we also experience a new mutual bond. When we stand around the altar, eat bread and drink wine, kneel in meditation, or walk in procession, we not only remember God's work in human history, but we also become aware of God's creative presence here and now. When we sit together in silent prayer, we create a space where we sense that the One we are waiting for is already touching us, as that One touched Elijah standing in front of the cave (1 Kings 19:13)....

Prayer as the language of the community is like our original tongue. Just as children learn to speak from their parents, brothers, sisters, and friends but still develop their own unique ways of expressing themselves, so also our individual prayer life develops by the care of the praying community. Sometimes it is hard to point to any specific organizational structure which we can call "our community." Our community is often a very intangible reality made up of people, living as well as dead, present as well as absent, close as well as distant, old as well as young. But without some form of community individual prayer cannot be born or developed. Communal and individual prayer belong together as two folded hands. Without community, individual prayer easily degenerates into egocentric and eccentric behavior, but without individual prayer, the prayer of the community quickly becomes a meaningless routine. Individual and community prayer cannot be separated without harm.   — Reaching Out

A New Way of Living

Precisely because we are so inclined to think in terms of individual greatness and personal heroism, it is important for us to reflect carefully on the fact that the compassionate life is community life. We witness to God's compassionate presence in the world by the way we live and work together. Those who were first converted by the Apostles revealed their conversion not by feats of individual stardom but by entering a new life in community: "The faithful all lived together and owned everything in common; they sold their goods and possessions and shared out the proceeds among themselves according to what each one needed. They went *as a body* to the Temple every day but met in their houses for the breaking of bread; they shared their food gladly and generously; they praised God and were looked up to by everyone" (Acts 2:44–47). God's compassion became evident in a radically new way of living, which so amazed and surprised outsiders that they said, "See how they love each other."

A compassionate life is a life in which fellowship with Christ reveals itself in a new fellowship among those who follow him. We tend so often to think of compassion as an individual accomplishment, that we easily lose sight of its essentially communal nature. By entering into fellowship with Jesus Christ, who emptied himself and became as we are and humbled himself by accepting death on the cross, we enter into a new relationship with each other. The new relationship with Christ and the new relationship with each other can never be separated. It is not enough to say that a new relationship with Christ leads to a new relationship with each other. Rather, we must say that the mind of Christ is the mind that gathers us together in community; our life in community is the manifestation of the mind of Christ.

—*Compassion*

Compassion and Community

To follow Christ means to relate to each other with the mind of Christ; that is, to relate to each other as Christ did to us — in servanthood and humility. Discipleship is walking together on the same path. While still living wholly *in* this world, we have discovered each other as fellow travelers on the same path and have formed a new community. While still subject to the power of the world and still deeply involved in the human struggle, we have become a new people with a new mind, a new way of seeing and hearing, and a new hope because of our common fellowship with Christ. Compassion, then, can never be separated from community. Compassion always reveals itself in community, in a new way of being together. Fellowship with Christ *is* fellowship with our brothers and sisters. This is most powerfully expressed by Paul when he calls the Christian community the body of Christ.

The presence of Jesus Christ, whose lordship resides in obedient service, manifests itself to us in the life of the Christian community. It is in the Christian community that we can be open and receptive to the suffering of the world and offer it a compassionate response. For where people come together in Christ's name, he is present as the compassionate Lord (see Matt. 18:20). Jesus Christ himself is and remains the most radical manifestation of God's compassion.

— *Compassion*

Mediators of the Unlimited Love of God

Community is the place where people give to one another. We are not God, but we can be mediators (in a limited way)

of the unlimited love of God. Community is the place of
joy and celebration where we can say to one another, "Be
of good cheer: the Lord has overcome the world, the Lord
has overcome the evil one. Do not be afraid." In that sense
the victory has already come. It is the victory of the cross,
it is the victory of the naked one on the cross, a victory
over death. Love is stronger than death, and community is
the place where you and I continue to let the world know
that there is something to celebrate, something to be joyful
about, something to be ecstatic about — ecstasy, *exstasis,* in
the sense of moving out of the static place of death. Community is the place from which we speak the Good News to
the world: "Don't be afraid. Look, it has already happened.
Christ is risen."
                                              — *The Road to Peace*

Obedience as a Communal Vocation

We must recognize that obedience, as an attentive listening
to God, is very much a communal vocation. It is precisely by
constant prayer and meditation that the community remains
alert and open to the needs of the world. Left to ourselves,
we might easily begin to idolize our particular form or style of
ministry and so turn our service into a personal hobby. But
when we come together regularly to listen to the word of God
and to celebrate God's presence in our midst, we stay alert
to God's guiding voice and move away from the comfortable
places to unknown territories. When we perceive obedience
as primarily a characteristic of the community itself, relationships between different members of a community can become
much more gentle. We also realize then that together we

want to discern God's will for us and make our service a response to God's compassionate presence in our midst.

— Compassion

The Discipline of Community

It may sound strange to speak of community as discipline, but without discipline community becomes a "soft" word, referring more to a safe, homey, and exclusive place than to the space where new life can be received and brought to its fullness. Wherever true community presents itself, discipline is crucial. It is crucial not only in the many old and new forms of the common life, but also in the sustaining relationships of friendship, marriage, and family. To create space for God among us requires the constant recognition of the Spirit of God in each other.

•

The discipline of community makes us persons; that is, people who are sounding through to each other (the Latin word *personare* means "sounding through") a truth, a beauty, and a love which are greater, fuller, and richer than we ourselves can grasp. In true community we are windows constantly offering each other new views on the mystery of God's presence in our lives. Thus the discipline of community is a true discipline of prayer. It makes us alert to the presence of the Spirit who cries out "Abba," Father, among us and thus prays from the center of our common life. Community thus is obedience practiced together.

The question is not simply, "Where does God lead me as an individual person who tries to do his will?" More basic and more significant is the question, "Where does God lead us as a people?" This question requires that we pay careful attention to God's guidance in our life together and that together we search for a creative response.   —*Making All Things New*

Community as a Quality of the Heart

We have to keep in mind that community, like solitude, is primarily a quality of the heart. While it remains true that we will never know what community is if we never come together in one place, community does not necessarily mean being physically together. We can well live in community while being physically alone. In such a situation, we can act freely, speak honestly, and suffer patiently, because of the intimate bond of love that unites us with others even when time and place separate us from them. The community of love stretches out not only beyond the boundaries of countries and continents but also beyond the boundaries of decades and centuries. Not only the awareness of those who are far away but also the memory of those who lived long ago can lead us into a healing, sustaining, and guiding community. The space for God in community transcends all limits of time and place.

Thus the discipline of community frees us to go wherever the Spirit guides us, even to places we would rather not go. This is the real Pentecost experience. When the Spirit descended on the disciples huddling together in fear, they were set free to move out of their closed room into the world. As long as they were assembled in fear they did not yet form community. But when they had received the Spirit, they became a body of free people who could stay in communion with each other even when they were as far from each other as Rome is from Jerusalem. Thus, when it is the Spirit of God and not fear that unites us in community, no distance of time or place can separate us.   —*Making All Things New*

The Community of Great Spiritual Men and Women

In the past, the saints had very much moved to the background of my consciousness. During the last few months, they re-entered my awareness as powerful guides on the way to God. I read the lives of many saints and great spiritual men and women, and it seems that they have become real members of my spiritual family, always present to offer suggestions, ideas, advice, consolation, courage, and strength. It is very hard to keep your heart and mind directed toward God when there are no examples to help you in your struggle. Without saints you easily settle for less-inspiring people and quickly follow the ways of others who for a while seem exciting but who are not able to offer lasting support. I am happy to have been able to restore my relationship with many great saintly men and women in history who, by their lives and works, can be real counselors to me.   —*The Genesee Diary*

The spiritual wisdom of many Christians, who in the course of history have dedicated their lives to prayer, is preserved and relived in the different traditions, lifestyles, or spiritualities that remain visible in contemporary Christianity. In fact, our first and most influential guides are often the prayer customs, styles of worship, and modes of speaking about God that pervade our different milieux. Each spiritual milieu has its own emphasis. . . . Much of the emphasis depends on the time in which a new spirituality found its beginning, on the personal character of the man or woman who was or is its main inspiration, and on the particular needs to which it responds.

The fact that these spiritualities are mostly related to influential historical personalities with great visibility helps us to use them as real guides in the search for our own personal way. Benedict, Francis, Dominic, Ignatius of Loyola, Teresa of Avila, Jacob Boehme, Francis de Sales, George Fox, John Wesley, Henry Martyn, John Henry Newman, Sören Kierkegaard, Charles de Foucauld, Dag Hammarskjöld, Martin Luther King, Jr., Thomas Merton, and many, many others offer us, by their own lives and the lives of their disciples and faithful students, a frame of reference and a point of orientation in our attempts to find the prayer of our heart. . . .

The really great saints of history don't ask for imitation. Their way was unique and cannot be repeated. But they invite us into their lives and offer a hospitable space for our own search. Some turn us off and make us feel uneasy; others even irritate us, but among the many great spiritual men and women in history we may find a few, or maybe just one or two, who speak the language of our heart and give us courage. These are our guides. Not to be imitated but to help us live our lives just as authentically as they lived theirs. When we have found such guides we have good reason to be grateful and even better reasons to listen attentively to what they have to say.   — *Reaching Out*

The Model of the Christian Community

Elizabeth and Mary came together [in Luke 1:39–56] and enabled each other to wait. Mary's visit made Elizabeth aware of what she was waiting for. The child leapt for joy in her. Mary affirmed Elizabeth's waiting. . . . I think that is the model of the Christian community. It is a community of support, celebration, and affirmation in which we can lift up what has already begun in us. The visit of Elizabeth and Mary is one of the Bible's most beautiful expressions of what it means to form community, to be together, gathered around a promise, affirming that something is really happening.

That is what prayer is all about. It is coming together around the promise. That is what celebration is all about. It is lifting up what is already there. That is what Eucharist is about. It is saying "Thanks" for the seed that has been planted. It is saying: "We are waiting for the Lord, who has already come."

The whole meaning of the Christian community lies in offering a space in which we wait for what we have already seen. Christian community is the place where we keep the flame alive among us and take it seriously, so that it can grow and become stronger in us. In this way we can live with courage, trusting that there is a spiritual power in us that allows us to live in this world without being seduced constantly by despair, lostness, and darkness. . . . Waiting together, nurturing what has already begun, expecting its fulfillment — that is the meaning of marriage, friendship, community, and the Christian life.   — "A Spirituality of Waiting"

Ten

Action and Intercession

To pray is to move to the center of all life and all love.

— Here and Now

Prayer and action...can never be seen as contradictory or mutually exclusive.

— Compassion

Connecting Prayer and Life

You must make the connection between prayer and life. The closer you are to the heart of God, the closer you come to the heart of the world, the closer you come to others. God is a demanding God, but when you give your heart to God, you find your heart's desires. You will also find your brother and sister right there. We're called always to action, but that action must not be driven, obsessive, or guilt-ridden. Basically, it's action that comes out of knowing God's love. You want to be with the poor because with them you're not trying to please the world and be accepted....

Our spirituality should come from living deeply with the poor. A spirituality of being with vulnerable people and of being vulnerable with them — that's the great journey!

— *The Road to Peace*

The discipline of patience reveals itself not only in the way we pray but also in the way we act. Our actions, like our prayers, must be a manifestation of God's compassionate presence in the midst of our world. Patient actions are actions through which the healing, consoling, comforting, reconciling, and unifying love of God can touch the heart of humanity. They are actions through which the fullness of time can show itself and God's justice and peace can guide our world. They are actions by which good news is brought to the poor, liberty to the prisoners, new sight to the blind, freedom to the oppressed, and God's year of favor is proclaimed (Luke 4:18–19). They are actions that remove the fear, suspicion, and power-hungry competition that cause an escalating arms race, an increasing separation between the wealthy and the poor, and an intensifying cruelty between the powerful and the powerless. They are actions that lead people to listen to each other, speak with each other, and heal each other's wounds. In short, they are actions based on a faith that knows God's presence in our lives and wants this presence to be felt by individuals, communities, societies, and nations.   —*Compassion*

Participating in God's Boundless Compassion

If it is true that a compassionate life is neither a series of good deeds by which we try to appease our guilt feelings toward our neighbors, nor a hectic attempt to do as much good as we possibly can, but rather participation in God's boundless compassion in and through Jesus Christ, then prayer is our first and in a certain sense only obligation. And this is so because prayer is a life in union with God, from whom all compassion flows.

Our call to compassion is not a call to try to find God in the heart of the world but to find the world in the heart of God. That is the way of Paul, Benedict, Francis, Ignatius, Teresa of Avila, Martin Luther, John Wesley, and all the spiritual leaders in the history of the Church. They all knew that the deeper our discipleship is, the deeper we enter into solidarity with the suffering world. There is nothing romantic, sweet, or easy about this. Those who think that this is a way out — or even a cop-out — do not know what it means to have the mind of Jesus Christ. There is little doubt anyone who enters to any degree into discipleship with Christ not only does not avoid the pain of the world, but penetrates into its center. That is why a life of prayer connects us in the most intimate way with the life of the world and that is why

in its final analysis a life of compassion is a mystical life — a
life lived in union with Jesus Christ.

— "Compassion: The Core of Spiritual Leadership"

Prayer and Acts of Service

Prayer and action ... can never be seen as contradictory or
mutually exclusive. Prayer without action grows into powerless pietism, and action without prayer degenerates into
questionable manipulation. If prayer leads us into a deeper
unity with the compassionate Christ, it will always give rise
to concrete acts of service. And if concrete acts of service do
indeed lead us to a deeper solidarity with the poor, the hungry, the sick, the dying, and the oppressed, they will always
give rise to prayer. In prayer we meet Christ, and in him all
human suffering. In service we meet people, and in them the
suffering Christ.   — *Compassion*

A Response of Gratitude

Compassionate action ... is the free, joyful, and, above all,
grateful manifestation of an encounter that has taken place.
The enormous energy with which John, Peter, Paul, and all
the disciples "conquered" their world with the message of
Jesus Christ came from that encounter. They did not have
to convince themselves or each other that they were doing
a good thing; they had no doubts concerning the value of
their work; they had no hesitation about the relevance of
their action. They could do nothing other than speak about
him, praise him, thank him, and worship him because it was

he whom they had heard, seen, and touched. They could do nothing other than bring light to the blind, freedom to the captives, and liberty to the oppressed because there they met him again. They could do nothing other than call people together into a new fellowship because thus he could be in their midst. Since Jesus Christ had become their true life, their true concern, their true compassion, and their true love, living became acting and all of life became an ongoing expression of thanks for God's great gift of himself.

This is the deepest meaning of compassionate action. It is the grateful, free, and joyful expression of the great encounter with the compassionate God. And it will be fruitful even when we can see neither how nor why. In and through such action, we realize that indeed all is grace and that our only possible response is gratitude.   —*Compassion*

Action as a Grateful Response

Action is a grateful response that flows from our awareness of God's presence in this world. Jesus' entire ministry was one great act of thanksgiving to his Father. It is to participation in this ministry that we are called. Peter and Paul traveled from place to place with a relentless energy; Teresa of Avila built convents as if she would never get tired; Martin Luther King, Jr., preached, planned, and organized with an unquenchable zeal, and Mother Teresa of Calcutta fearlessly [hastened] the coming of the Lord with her care for the poorest of the poor. But none of them tried to solve the problems of the world or sought to gather praise or prizes. Their actions were free from these compulsions, and consequently were spontaneous responses to the experience of God's active presence in their lives. Thus our action can become thanksgiving, and all that we do can become Eucharist.   — "Contemplation and Action"

Acting within the House of God

Here too we find the ground of all Christian action. As prayer leads us into the house of God and God's people, so action leads us back into the world to work there for reconciliation, unity, and peace. Once we have come to know the truth, we want to act truthfully and reveal to the world its true nature. All Christian action — whether it is visiting the sick, feeding the hungry, clothing the naked, or working for a more just and peaceful society — is a manifestation of the human solidarity revealed to us in the house of God. It is not an anxious human effort to create a better world. It is a confident expression of the truth that in Christ, death, evil, and destruction have been overcome. It is not a fearful attempt to restore a broken order. It is a joyful assertion that in Christ all order has already been restored. It is not a nervous effort to bring divided people together, but a celebration of an already established unity. Thus action is not activism. An activist wants to heal, restore, redeem, and re-create, but those acting within the house of God point through their action to the healing, restoring, redeeming, and re-creating presence of God.   — *Lifesigns*

Actions That Bring Joy and Peace

Action...can help us to claim and celebrate our true self. But here again we need discipline, because the world in which we live says: "Do this, do that, go here, go there, meet him, meet her." Busyness has become a sign of importance. Having much to do, many places to go, and countless people to meet gives us status and even fame. However, being busy can lead us away from our true vocation and prevent us from drinking our cup.

It is not easy to distinguish between doing what we are called to do and doing what we want to do. Our many wants can easily distract us from our true action. True action leads us to the fulfillment of our vocation.... The most prestigious position in society can be an expression of obedience to our call as well as a sign of our refusal to hear that call, and the least prestigious position, too, can be a response to our vocation as well as a way to avoid it.

Drinking our cup involves carefully choosing those actions which lead us closer to complete emptying of it, so that at the end of our lives we can say with Jesus: "It is fulfilled" (John 19:30). That indeed, is the paradox: we fulfill life by emptying it. In Jesus' own words: "Anyone who loses his life for my sake will find it" (Matt. 10:39).

When we are committed to do God's will and not our own we soon discover that much of what we do doesn't need to be done by us. What we are called to do are actions that bring us true joy and peace. Just as leaving friends for the sake of the Gospel will bring us friends, so too will letting go of actions not in accord with our call.

Actions that lead to overwork, exhaustion, and burnout can't praise and glorify God. What God calls us to do we *can* do and do *well*. When we listen in silence to God's voice and speak with our friends in trust we will know what we are called to do, and we will do it with a grateful heart.

—*Can You Drink the Cup?*

Compassionate Prayer

Compassionate prayer on behalf of others is central to the Bible. Abraham intercedes for the inhabitants of Sodom and Gomorrah and thereby saves them from God's anger (Gen. 18:32). When the Israelites break the covenant of Mt. Sinai by worshiping the golden calf, it is only the intercession of Moses that prevents their destruction (Exod. 32:11–14)....

As disciples of the compassionate Lord who took upon himself the condition of a slave and suffered death for our sake, there are no boundaries to our prayers. Dietrich Bonhoeffer expressed this with powerful simplicity when he wrote that to pray for others is to give them "the same right we have received, namely, to stand before Christ and share in his mercy."

When we come before God with the needs of the world, then the healing love of God which touches us touches all those whom we bring before him with the same power. This experience of God's healing love can become so real, so immediate, that at times we can even sense God's healing grace in the lives of others, although they may be far away physically, mentally, or spiritually.

Thus, compassionate prayer does not encourage us to flee from people and their concrete problems into a self-serving individualism. By deepening our awareness of our common suffering, it draws us all closer together in the healing presence of God. It reaches out not only to those whom we love and admire, but also to those whom we consider our enemies.

Prayer cannot exist together with hostile feelings. The fruit of prayer is always love. In prayer, even the unprincipled dictator and the vicious torturer can no longer remain the objects of our fear, hatred, and revenge, because when we pray, we stand at the center of the great mystery of divine compassion.   — "Anchored in God through Prayer"

Pray for One Another

We often wonder what we can do for others, especially for those in great need. It is not a sign of powerlessness when we say: "We must pray for one another." To pray for one another is, first of all, to acknowledge, in the presence of God, that we belong to each other as children of the same God. Without this acknowledgment of human solidarity, what we do for one another does not flow from who we truly are. We are brothers and sisters, not competitors or rivals. We are children of one God, not partisans of different gods.

To pray, that is, to listen to the voice of the One who calls us the "Beloved," is to learn that that voice excludes no one. Where I dwell, God dwells with me and where God dwells with me I find all my sisters and brothers. And so intimacy with God and solidarity with all people are two aspects of dwelling in the present moment that can never be separated.

— *Here and Now*

Making Others Part of Ourselves

One of the most powerful experiences in a life of compassion is the expansion of our hearts into a world-embracing space of healing from which no one is excluded. When, through discipline, we have overcome the power of our impatient impulses to flee or to fight, to become fearful or angry, we discover a limitless space into which we can welcome all the people of the world. Prayer for others, therefore, cannot be seen as an extraordinary exercise that must be practiced from time to time. Rather, it is the very beat of a compassionate heart. To pray for a friend who is ill, for a student who is depressed, for a teacher who is in conflict; for people in prisons, in hospitals, on battlefields; for those who are victims of injustice, who are hungry, poor, and without shelter; for those who risk their career, their health, and even their life in the struggle for social justice; for leaders of church and state — to pray for all these people is not a futile effort to influence God's will, but a hospitable gesture by which we invite our neighbors into the center of our hearts.

To pray for others means to make them part of ourselves. To pray for others means to allow their pains and sufferings, their anxieties and loneliness, their confusion and fears to resound in our innermost selves. To pray, therefore, is to become those for whom we pray, to become the sick child, the fearful mother, the distressed father, the nervous teenager, the angry student, and the frustrated striker. To pray is to enter into a deep inner solidarity with our fellow human beings so that in and through us they can be touched by the healing power of God's Spirit. When, as disciples of Christ, we are able to bear the burdens of our brothers and sisters, to be marked with their wounds, and even be broken by their sins, our prayer becomes their prayer, our cry for mercy becomes their cry. In compassionate prayer, we bring before God those who suffer not merely "over there," not simply "long ago," but here and now in our innermost selves. And so it is in and through us that others are restored; it is in and through us that they receive new light, new hope, and new courage; it is in and through us that the Spirit touches them with God's healing presence. —*Compassion*

When I really bring my friends and the many I pray for into my innermost being and feel their pains, their struggles, their cries in my own soul, then I leave myself, so to speak, and become them, then I have compassion. Compassion lies at the heart of our prayer for our fellow human beings. When I pray for the world, I become the world; when I pray for the endless needs of the millions, my soul expands and wants to embrace them all and bring them into the presence of God. But in the midst of that experience I realize that compassion is not mine but God's gift to me. I cannot embrace the world, but God can. I cannot pray, but God can pray in me. When God became as we are, that is, when God allowed all of us to enter into his intimate life, it became possible for us to share in his infinite compassion.

In praying for others, I lose myself and become the other, only to be found by the divine love which holds the whole of humanity in a compassionate embrace.   — *The Genesee Diary*

Communion with the People of God

What I would like you to see is that if you come in touch with that first love you will discover not only that you are loved unconditionally, but that the One who loves you unconditionally loves all of humanity unconditionally, with that same all-embracing love. And the fact that God loves you so intimately and personally does not mean that God loves anyone else less or differently. Uniquely, yes. But whether they are Nicaraguans or Russians, people from Afghanistan or Iran or South Africa, they all belong to the house of God. And therefore, when you enter into intimate communion with the God of the first love, you will find yourself in intimate communion with all the people of God, because the heart of God is the heart that embraces the whole of humanity. That's why intimacy with God always means solidarity with the people of God. To put it more precisely: God pitched a tent among us and took on our flesh so that there is no human flesh that has not been accepted by God. Therefore, prayer is not just communion with God in the privacy of your own place. It is communion with the people of God over the centuries and around the world that gives you a sense of belonging, a sense of overcoming the fear that separates you; it is that communion that sets you free. — *The Road to Peace*

Moving to the Hub of Life

In my home country, the Netherlands, you still see many large wagon wheels . . . as decorations. . . . I have always been fascinated by these wagon wheels. . . . These wheels help me to understand the importance of a life lived from the center. When I move along the rim, I can reach one spoke after the other, but when I stay at the hub, I am in touch with all the spokes at once.

To pray is to move to the center of all life and all love. The closer I come to the hub of life, the closer I come to all that receives its strength and energy from there. My tendency is to get so distracted by the diversity of the many spokes of life, that I am busy but not truly life-giving, all over the place but not focused. By directing my attention to the heart of life, I am connected with its rich variety while remaining centered. What does the hub represent? I think of it as my own heart, the heart of God, and the heart of the world. When I pray, I enter into the depth of my own heart and find there the heart of God, who speaks to me of love. And I recognize, right there, the place where all of my sisters and brothers are in communion with one another. The great paradox of the spiritual life is, indeed, that the most personal is most universal, that the most intimate is most communal, and that the most contemplative is most active.

The wagon wheel shows that the hub is the center of all energy and movement, even when it often seems not to be moving at all. In God all action and all rest are one. So too prayer!   —*Here and Now*

Eleven

Forgiveness

We need to forgive and be forgiven every day, every
hour — unceasingly.

— "Forgiveness: The Name of Love in a Wounded World"

Forgiveness means that I continually am willing to
forgive the other person for not being God — for
not fulfilling all my needs.   — "Parting Words"

Forgiving in the Name of God

We are all wounded people. Who wounds us? Often those
whom we love and those who love us. When we feel rejected,
abandoned, abused, manipulated, or violated, it is mostly by
people very close to us: our parents, our friends, our spouses,
our lovers, our children, our neighbors, our teachers, our pas-
tors. Those who love us wound us too. That's the tragedy
of our lives. This is what makes forgiveness from the heart
so difficult. It is precisely our hearts that are wounded. We
cry out, "You, who I expected to be there for me, you have
abandoned me. How can I ever forgive you for that?"

Forgiveness often seems impossible, but nothing is impossible for God. The God who lives within us will give us the
grace to go beyond our wounded selves and say, "In the
Name of God you are forgiven."   —*Bread for the Journey*

Forgiving People for Not Being God

Forgiveness means that I continually am willing to forgive
the other person for not being God — for not fulfilling all
my needs. I, too, must ask forgiveness for not being able to
fulfill other people's needs. Our heart — the center of our being — is a part of God. Thus, our heart longs for satisfaction,
for total communion. But human beings, whether it's your
husband, or your wife, or your father, or your mother, your
brother, sister, or child, they are all so limited in giving that
which we crave. But since we want so much and we get only
part of what we want, we have to keep on forgiving people
for not giving us all we want. . . .

The interesting thing is that when you can forgive people

for not being God then you can celebrate that they are a reflection of God. You can say, "Since you are not God, I love you because you have such beautiful gifts of God's love." You don't have everything of God, but what you have to offer is worth celebrating. By celebrate I mean to lift up, affirm, confirm, to rejoice in another person's gifts. You can say you are a reflection of that unlimited love.   — "Parting Words"

The First Movement of the Dance with God

Healing begins not where our pain is taken away, but where it can be shared and seen as part of a larger pain. The first task of healing, therefore, is to take our many problems and pains out of their isolation and place them at the center of the great battle against the Evil One.... As we create the space to mourn — whether through one-to-one relationships, small support groups, or communal celebrations — we free ourselves little by little from the grip of the Evil One and come to discover in the midst of our grief that the same Spirit who calls us to mourn stirs us to make the first movement in our dance with God....

Let me describe... the movements of the dance. Let me be your dance master for a while! The first movement is forgiveness. It's a very difficult movement. But, then, all beginnings are difficult, and there is so much forgiving to do. We have to forgive our parents for not being able to give us unconditional love, our brothers and sisters for not giving us the support we dreamt about, our friends for not being there for us when we expected them. We have to forgive our church and civil leaders for their ambitions and manipulations. Beyond all that, we have to forgive all those who torture, kill, rape, destroy — who make this world such a dark place. And we, ourselves, also have to beg forgiveness. The older we become, the more clearly we see that we, too, have wounded others deeply, and are part of a society of violence and destruction. It is very difficult to forgive and to ask for forgiveness. But, without this, we remain fettered to our past — unable to dance....

Forgiveness is the great spiritual weapon against the Evil One. As long as we remain victims of anger and resentment, the power of darkness can continue to divide us and tempt us with endless power games. But when we forgive those who threaten our lives, they lose their power over us.... Forgiveness enables us to take the first step of the dance.   — "The Duet of the Holy Spirit:
                                        When Mourning and Dancing Are One"

Taking the Step of Forgiveness

Forgiveness is made possible by the knowledge that human beings cannot offer us what only God can give. Once we have heard the voice calling us the Beloved, accepted the gift of full communion, and claimed the first unconditional love, we can see easily — with the eyes of a repentant heart — how we have demanded of people a love that only God can give. It is the knowledge of that first love that allows us to forgive those who have only a "second" love to offer.

I am struck by how I cling to my own wounded self. Why do I think so much about the people who have offended or hurt me? Why do I allow them to have so much power over my feelings and emotions? Why can't I simply be grateful for the good they did and forget about their failures and mistakes? It seems that in order to find my place in life I need to be angry, resentful, or hurt. It even seems that these people gave me my identity by the very ways in which they wounded me. Part of me is "the wounded one." It is hard to know who I am when I can no longer point my finger at someone who is the cause of my pain! . . .

It is important to understand our suffering. It is often necessary to search for the origins of our mental and emotional struggles and to discover how other people's actions and our response to their actions have shaped the way we think, feel, and act. Most of all, it is freeing to become aware that we do not have to be victims of our past and can learn new ways of responding. But there is a step beyond the recognition and identification of the facts of life. There is even a step beyond choosing how to live our own life story. It is the greatest step a human being can take. It is the step of forgiveness.

Forgiveness is the name of love practiced among people who love poorly. The hard truth is that all of us love poorly. We do not even know what we are doing when we hurt others. We need to forgive and be forgiven every day, every hour — unceasingly. That is the great work of love among the fellowship of the weak that is the human family. The voice that calls us the Beloved is the voice of freedom because it sets us free to love without wanting anything in return. This has nothing to do with self-sacrifice, self-denial, or self-deprecation. But it has everything to do with the abundance of love that has been freely given to me and from which I freely want to give.

— "Forgiveness: The Name of Love in a Wounded World"

Praying for Our Enemies

The first thing we are called to do when we think of others as
our enemies is to pray for them. This is certainly not easy. It
requires discipline to allow those who hate us or those toward
whom we have hostile feelings to come into the intimate center of our hearts. People who make our lives difficult and
cause us frustration, pain, or even harm are least likely to receive a place in our hearts. Yet every time we overcome this
impatience with our opponents and are willing to listen to
the cry of those who persecute us, we will recognize them as
brothers and sisters too. Praying for our enemies is therefore
a real event, the event of reconciliation. It is impossible to lift
our enemies up in the presence of God and at the same time
continue to hate them. . . . Prayer converts the enemy into a
friend and is thus the beginning of a new relationship. There
is probably no prayer as powerful as the prayer for our enemies. But it is also the most difficult prayer since it is most
contrary to our impulses. This explains why some saints consider prayer for our enemies the main criterion of holiness.

—*Compassion*

If you wish to learn the love of God, you have to begin
by praying for your enemies. That's not as easy as it may
sound. Prayers for people entail wanting the best for them;
and that's far from easy if it has to do with a fellow student
who speaks ill of you, a girl who finds someone else more
attractive than you, a "friend" who gets you to do all those
awkward little chores for him, or a colleague who's trying
his best to get your job. But each time you pray, really pray,
for your enemies, you'll notice that your heart is being made
new. Within your prayer, you quickly discover that your en-

emies are in fact your fellow human beings loved by God just as much as yourself. The result is that the walls you've thrown up between "him and me," "us and them," "ours and theirs" disappear. Your heart grows deeper and broader and opens up more and more to all the human beings with whom God has peopled the earth.

I find it difficult to conceive of a more concrete way to love than by praying for one's enemies. It makes you conscious of the hard fact that, in God's eyes, you're no more and no less worthy of being loved than any other person, and it creates an awareness of profound solidarity with all other human beings. It creates in you a world-embracing compassion and provides you in increasing measure with a heart free of the compulsive urge to coercion and violence. And you'll be delighted to discover that you can no longer remain angry with people for whom you've really and truly prayed. You will find that you start speaking differently to them or about them, and that you're actually willing to do well to those who've offended you in some way.

—*Letters to Marc about Jesus*

The Two Qualities of Forgiveness

Forgiveness has two qualities: one is to allow yourself to be forgiven, and the other is to forgive others. The first quality is harder than the second. To allow yourself to be forgiven puts you in a dependency situation. If someone says to me, "I want to forgive you for something," I may say back, "But I didn't do anything. I don't need forgiveness. Get out of my life." It's very important that we acknowledge that we are not fulfilling other people's needs and that we need to be forgiven. There is great resistance to that. We come from a culture that is terribly damaged in this area. We find it hard to forgive or ask to be forgiven.... It's not just individuals who need to forgive and be forgiven. We all need to be forgiven. We ask each other to put ourselves in that vulnerable position — and that's when community can be created.

— "Parting Words"

God's Eagerness to Forgive

Forgiveness from the heart is very, very difficult. It is next to impossible. Jesus said to his disciples: "When your brother wrongs you seven times a day and seven times comes back to you and says, 'I am sorry,' you must forgive him." I have often said, "I forgive you," but even as I said these words my heart remained angry or resentful. I still wanted to hear the story that tells me that I was right after all; I still wanted to hear apologies and excuses; I still wanted the satisfaction of receiving some praise in return — if only the praise for being so forgiving!

But God's forgiveness is unconditional; it comes from a heart that does not demand anything for itself, a heart that is completely empty of self-seeking. It is this divine forgiveness that I have to practice in my daily life. It calls me to keep stepping over all my arguments that say forgiveness is unwise, unhealthy, and impractical. It challenges me to step over all my needs for gratitude and compliments. Finally, it demands of me that I step over that wounded part of my heart that feels hurt and wronged and that wants to stay in control and put a few conditions between me and the one whom I am asked to forgive.   *— The Return of the Prodigal Son*

The Healing Calm of God's Forgiveness

When I read [Psalm 42] last Monday during my morning prayer, I noticed that the psalm-prayer that followed it entered into my soul with an unusual power, so much so that it has stayed with me during the last few days. The prayer says:

Father in heaven, when your strength takes possession of us we no longer say: Why are you cast down, my soul? So now that the surging waves of our indignation have passed over us, let us feel the healing calm of your forgiveness. Inspire us to yearn for you always, like the deer for running streams, until you satisfy every longing in heaven.

The words "let us feel the healing calm of your forgiveness" are words that I want to hold on to, because if I desire anything, it is the healing calm of God's forgiveness. The longer I live, the more I am aware of my sinfulness, faithlessness, lack of courage, narrow-mindedness; the more I feel the surging waves of greed, lust, violence, and indignation roaring in my innermost self. Growing older has not made life with God easier. In fact, it has become harder to experience God's presence, to feel God's love, to taste God's goodness, to touch God's caring hands. Oh, how much do I pray that God will let me know through all my senses that God's love is more real than my sins and my cowardice, how much do I want to see the light in darkness, and how much do I wait for the day that God will order the surging waves to calm down, and how much do I wait to hear God's voice, which says: "Why are you afraid, man of little faith? I am with you always." — *¡Gracias!*

Confession and Forgiveness

Everyone is a different refraction of the same love of God, the same light of the world, coming to us. We need a contemplative discipline for seeing this light. We can't see God in the world, only God can see God in the world. That is why contemplative life is so essential for the active ministry. If I have discovered God as the center of my being, then the God in me recognizes God in the world. We also then recognize the demons at work in us and the world. The demons are always close, trying to conquer us. The spiritual life requires a constant and vigilant deepening and enlivening of the presence of God in our hearts.

This process includes the real tension of discerning with which eye I see God: my own eye that wants to please and control, or God's eye. Life therefore needs to be lived in an ongoing process of confession and forgiveness. This is the ongoing dynamic of community. The demons lose their power when we confess that we have been in their clutches. The more deeply we confess, the more we will experience the forgiving love of God — and the more deeply we will realize how much more we have to confess. Community life encourages this confession of our demons and our enchantment with them, so that the love of God can reveal itself. Only in confession will the Good News be revealed to us, as the New Testament with its focus on sinners makes clear.

— *The Road to Peace*

The Embrace of a Forgiving God

To pray means to stop expecting from God the same small-mindedness which you discover in yourself. To pray is to walk in the full light of God and to say simply, without holding back, "I am human and you are God." At that moment, conversion occurs, the restoration of the true relationship. A human being is not someone who once in a while makes a mistake, and God is not someone who now and then forgives. No! Human beings are sinners and God is love. . . . This conversion brings with it the relaxation which lets you breathe again and puts you at rest in the embrace of a forgiving God.

—*With Open Hands*

Twelve

Hindrances

It is precisely in times of spiritual dryness that we must hold on to our spiritual discipline so that we can grow into new intimacy with God.

— Bread for the Journey

Often you will feel that nothing happens in your prayer. You say: "I am just sitting there and getting distracted."

— Life of the Beloved

Spiritual Dryness

Sometimes we experience a terrible dryness in our spiritual lives. We feel no desire to pray, don't experience God's presence, get bored with worship services, and even think that everything we ever believed about God, Jesus, and the Holy Spirit is little more than a childhood fairy tale.

Then it is important to realize that most of these feelings and thoughts are just feelings and thoughts, and that the Spirit of God dwells beyond our feelings and thoughts. It is a great grace to be able to experience God's presence in our feelings and thoughts, but when we don't, it does not mean that God is absent. It often means that God is calling us to a greater faithfulness. It is precisely in times of spiritual dryness that we must hold on to our spiritual discipline so that we can grow into new intimacy with God. —*Bread for the Journey*

So, what about my life of prayer? Do I like to pray? Do I want to pray? Do I spend time praying? Frankly, the answer is no to all three questions. After sixty-three years of life and thirty-eight years of priesthood, my prayer seems as dead as a rock. I remember fondly my teenage years, when I could hardly stay away from the church. For hours I would stay on my knees filled with a deep sense of Jesus' presence. I couldn't believe that not everyone wanted to pray. Prayer was so intimate and so satisfying. It was during these prayer-filled years that my vocation to the priesthood was shaped. During the years that followed I have paid much attention to prayer, reading about it, writing about it, visiting monasteries and houses of prayer, and guiding many people on their spiritual journeys. By now I should be full of spiritual fire, consumed by prayer.

Many people think I am and speak to me as if prayer is my greatest gift and deepest desire.

The truth is that I do not feel much, if anything, when I pray. There are no warm emotions, bodily sensations, or mental visions. None of my five senses is being touched — no special smells, no special sounds, no special sights, no special tastes, and no special movements. Whereas for a long time the Spirit acted so clearly through my flesh, now I feel nothing. I have lived with the expectation that prayer would become easier as I grow older and closer to death. But the opposite seems to be happening. The words "darkness" and "dryness" seem to best describe my prayer today.

Maybe part of this darkness and dryness is the result of my overactivity. As I grow older I become busier and spend less and less time in prayer. But I probably should not blame myself in that way. The real questions are, "What are the darkness and the dryness about? What do they call me to?..." I know that Jesus, at the end of his life, felt abandoned by God. "My God, my God," he cried out on the cross, "why have you forsaken me?" (Matt. 27:46). His body had been destroyed by his torturers, his mind was no longer able to grasp the meaning of his existence, and his soul was void of any consolation. Still, it was from his broken heart that water and blood, signs of new life, came out.

Are the darkness and dryness of my prayer signs of God's absence, or are they signs of a presence deeper and wider than my senses can contain? Is the death of my prayer the end of my intimacy with God or the beginning of a new communion, beyond words, emotions, and bodily sensations?

As I sit down for half an hour to be in the presence of God and to pray, not much is happening.... Still, maybe this time is a way of dying with Jesus.
                                                            — *Sabbatical Journey*

My long journey has harmed my prayer life. I have discovered how hard it has become for me to spend one hour in the morning simply being present to Jesus. I experience a certain nausea or apathy that I did not have before I left. It is a sort of spiritual fatigue, a state of lukewarmness in which I find it hard to know exactly what I feel, what I think, or what I want. It is like being a piece of driftwood on still water. Nothing seems to move, and there seems to be no way to get things moving again. I am tired, but I do not sleep well. I am talking to people, but I do not feel well connected. I do many things, but not much is happening. I do not feel depressed, just empty and somewhat indifferent. Maybe it is a temporary "burnout." Well, I am not panicky about it and try to stay in touch with Jesus. What helps me most is praying with others. I very much enjoy saying my morning and evening prayers with friends, and I am very grateful when Nathan prays with me. Friends keep me close to Jesus. I just have to drink in their love and let them pray with and for me.

— *The Road to Daybreak*

From Unceasing Thinking to Unceasing Prayer

Our minds are always active. We analyze, reflect, daydream, or dream. There is not a moment during the day or night when we are not thinking. You might say our thinking is "unceasing." Sometimes we wish that we could stop thinking for a while; that would save us from many worries, guilt feelings, and fears. Our ability to think is our greatest gift, but it is also the source of our greatest pain. Do we have to become victims of our unceasing thoughts? No, we can convert our unceasing thinking into unceasing prayer by making our inner monologue into a continuing dialogue with our God, who is the source of all love.

Let's break out of our isolation and realize that Someone who dwells in the center of our beings wants to listen with love to all that occupies and preoccupies our minds.

— *Bread for the Journey*

Intellect as a Hindrance

This week all I am reading and writing about is prayer. I am so busy with it and often so excited about it that I have no time left to pray, and when I pray, I feel more drawn to my ideas on prayer than to praying....

I have a strong feeling that my intellectual formation is just as much a hindrance as a help to prayer. It is hard not to desire good insights during prayer and not to fall into a long inner discussion with myself. Every time some kind of insight comes to me, I find myself wondering how I can use it in a lecture, a sermon, or an article, and very soon I am far away from God and all wrapped up in my own preoccupations. Maybe this is what makes the Jesus Prayer so good for me. Simply saying, "Lord Jesus Christ, have mercy on me" a hundred times, a thousand times, ten thousand times, as the Russian peasant did, might slowly clean my mind and give God a little chance.

— *The Genesee Diary*

From Worrying to Prayer

One of the least helpful ways to stop worrying is to try hard not to think about the things we are worrying about. We can-

not push away our worries with our minds.... Jesus' advice
to set our hearts on God's kingdom is somewhat paradoxi-
cal. You might give it the following interpretation: "If you
want to worry, worry about that which is worth the effort.
Worry about larger things than your family, your friends, or
tomorrow's meeting. Worry about the things of God: truth,
life, and light!"

As soon, however, as we set our hearts on these things
our minds stop spinning because we enter into communion
with the One who is present to us here and now and is there
to give us what we most need. And so worrying becomes
prayer, and our feelings of powerlessness are transformed into
a consciousness of being empowered by God's Spirit....

Does that put an end to our worrying? Probably not. As
long as we are in our world, full of tensions and pressures, our
minds will never be free from worries, but when we keep returning with our hearts and minds to God's embracing love,
we will be able to keep smiling at our own worrisome selves
and keep our eyes and ears open for the sights and sounds of
the kingdom.   *—Here and Now*

One of the most notable characteristics of worrying is that it
fragments our lives. The many things to do, to think about,
to plan for, the many people to remember, to visit, or to talk
with, the many causes to attack or defend, all these pull us
apart and make us lose our center. Worrying causes us to be
"all over the place," but seldom at home.... We know where
we belong, but we keep being pulled away in many directions,
as if we were still homeless. "All these other things" keep
demanding our attention. They lead us so far from home that
we eventually forget our true address, that is, the place where
we can be addressed.

Jesus responds to this condition of being filled yet unful-filled, very busy yet unconnected, all over the place yet never at home. He wants to bring us to the place where we belong. But his call to live a spiritual life can be heard only when we are willing honestly to confess our own homeless and wor-rying existence and recognize its fragmenting effect on our daily life. Only then can a desire for our true home develop. It is of this desire that Jesus speaks when he says, "Do not worry.... Set your hearts on his kingdom first ... and all these others things will be given you as well."

— *Making All Things New*

What to Do with Distractions

But what to do with our many distractions? Should we fight these distractions and hope that thus we will become more attentive to God's voice? This does not seem the way to come to prayer. Creating an empty space where we can listen to God's Spirit is not easy when we are putting all our energy into fighting distractions. By fighting distractions in such a direct way, we end up paying more attention to them than they deserve.

We have, however, the words of Scripture to which to pay attention. A psalm, a parable, a biblical story, a saying of Jesus, or a word of Paul, Peter, James, Jude, or John can help us to focus our attention on God's presence. Thus we deprive those "many other things" of their power over us. When we place words from the Scriptures in the center of our solitude, such words — whether a short expression, a few sentences, or a longer text — can function as the point to which we return when we have wandered off in different directions. They form a safe anchoring place in a stormy sea.

—*Making All Things New*

Befriending Our Inner Enemies

How do we befriend our inner enemies lust and anger? By listening to what they are saying. They say, "I have some unfulfilled needs" and "Who really loves me?" Instead of pushing our lust and anger away as unwelcome guests, we can recognize that our anxious, driven hearts need some healing. Our restlessness calls us to look for the true inner rest where lust and anger can be converted into a deeper way of loving.

There is a lot of unruly energy in lust and anger! When that energy can be directed toward loving well, we can transform not only ourselves but even those who might otherwise become the victims of our anger and lust. This takes patience, but it is possible. —*Bread for the Journey*

Being Free from All Fear

Jesus came to us to help us overcome our fear of God. As long as we are afraid of God, we cannot love God. Love means intimacy, closeness, mutual vulnerability, and a deep sense of safety. But all of those are impossible as long as there is fear. Fear creates suspicion, distance, defensiveness, and insecurity.

The greatest block in the spiritual life is fear. Prayer, meditation, and education cannot come forth out of fear. God is perfect love, and as John the Evangelist writes, "Perfect love drives out fear" (1 John 4:18). Jesus' central message is that God loves us with an unconditional love and desires our love, free from all fear, in return.   —*Bread for the Journey*

To those who are tortured by inner or outer fear, and who desperately look for the house of love where they can find the intimacy their hearts desire, Jesus says: "You have a home...I am your home...claim me as your home...you will find it to be the intimate place where I have found my home...it is right where you are...in your innermost being...in your heart." The more attentive we are to such words the more we realize that we do not have to go far to find what we are searching for.

The tragedy is that we are so possessed by fear that we do not trust our innermost self as an intimate place but anxiously wander around hoping to find it where we are not. We try to find that intimate place in knowledge, competence, notoriety, success, friends, sensations, pleasure, dreams, or artificially induced states of consciousness. Thus we become strangers to ourselves, people who have an address but are never home and hence can never be addressed by the true voice of love.   —*Lifesigns*

The ark is a house that rocks and rolls on the waves of our times. Nobody remains without some fear. But Jesus is in the ark, asleep! He is close to us. Whenever the fear becomes overwhelming and we wake him up anxiously, saying: "Save us, Lord, we are going down," he says: "Why are you so frightened, you people of little faith?" Then he rebukes the winds and sea and makes all calm again (see Matt. 8:23–27). The ark is our home, and Jesus has made it his own. He travels with us and continues to reassure us every time we are driven to panic or tempted to destroy others or ourselves. And as he travels with us, he teaches us how to live in the house of love. It is far from easy to grasp his teaching because we keep looking at the high waves, the heavy winds, and the roaring storm. We keep saying: "Yes, yes . . . but look!"

Jesus is a very patient teacher. He never stops telling us where to make our true home, what to look for, and how to live. When we are distracted, we focus upon all the dangers and forget what we have heard. But Jesus says over and over again: "Make your home in me, as I make mine in you. Whoever remains in me, with me in them, bears fruit in plenty . . . I have told you this so that my own joy may be in you, and your joy may be complete" (John 15:4, 5, 11). Thus, Jesus invites us to an intimate, fruitful, and ecstatic life in his home, which is ours too.   —*Lifesigns*

Overcoming Mood Swings

Are we condemned to be passive victims of our moods? Must we simply say, "I feel great today" or "I feel awful today," and require others to live with our moods?

Although it is very hard to control our moods, we can gradually overcome them by living a well-disciplined spiritual life. This can prevent us from acting out of our moods. We might not "feel" like getting up in the morning because we "feel" that life is not worth living, that nobody loves us, and that our work is boring. But if we get up anyhow, to spend some time reading the Gospels, praying the Psalms, and thanking God for a new day, our moods may lose their power over us.   —*Bread for the Journey*

When Prayer Seems Useless

Why should I spend an hour in prayer when I do nothing during that time but think about people I am angry with, people who are angry with me, books I should read and books I should write, and thousands of other silly things that happen to grab my mind for a moment? The answer is: because God is greater than my mind and my heart, and what is really happening in the house of prayer is not measurable in terms of human success and failure.

What I must do first of all is be faithful. If I believe that the first commandment is to love God with my whole heart, mind, and soul, then I should at least be able to spend one hour a day with nobody else but God. The question as to whether it is helpful, useful, practical, or fruitful is completely irrelevant, since the only reason to love is love itself. Everything else is secondary.

The remarkable thing, however, is that sitting in the presence of God for one hour each morning — day after day, week after week, month after month — in total confusion and with myriad distractions radically changes my life. God, who loves me so much that he sent his only Son not to condemn me but to save me, does not leave me waiting in the dark too long. I might think that each hour is useless, but after thirty or sixty or ninety such useless hours, I gradually realize that I was not as alone as I thought; a very small, gentle voice has been speaking to me far beyond my noisy place.

So: Be confident and trust in the Lord.

— *The Road to Daybreak*

Prayer continues to be very difficult. Still, every morning when I walk in the garden of La Ferme saying the rosary and spending an hour in the oratory simply being in God's presence, I know that I am not wasting my time. Though I am terribly distracted, I know that God's Spirit is at work in me. Though I have no deeply religious insights or feelings, I am aware of the peace beyond thoughts and emotions. Though my early-morning prayer seems quite unsuccessful, I always look forward to it and guard it as a special time.

A short piece on prayer by Dom John Chapman published in the December 14th *Tablet* has given me much hope. It is taken from one of his spiritual letters.... The sentence that I like most is, "The only way to pray is to pray; and the way to pray well is to pray much."[1] Chapman's sound wisdom really helps me. No-nonsense advice, and very true. It all boils down to his main point: We must pray not first of all because it feels good or helps, but because God loves us and wants our attention.   — *The Road to Daybreak*

One of the experiences of prayer is that it seems that nothing happens. But when you stay with it and look back over a long period of prayer, you suddenly realize that something has happened. What is most close, most intimate, most present, often cannot be experienced directly but only with a certain distance. When I think that I am only distracted, just wasting my time, something is happening too immediate for knowing, understanding, and experiencing. Only in retrospect do I realize that something very important has taken place. Isn't this true of all really important events in life? ...

---

1. *The Spiritual Letters of Dom John Chapman*, O.S.B. (London: Sheed and Ward, 1938), 52–53; quoted in *The Tablet*, December 14, 1985.

When I think about prayer, I can talk about it with moving words and write about it with conviction, but in both situations I am not really praying but reflecting on it with a certain distance. But when I pray, my prayer often seems very confused, dull, uninspiring, and distracted. God is close but often too close to experience. God is closer to me than I am to myself and, therefore, no subject for feelings or thoughts.

I wonder if in this sense I am not participating in what the apostles experienced. When Jesus was with them, they could not fully realize or understand what was happening. Only after he had left did they sense, feel, and understand how close he really had been to them. Their experience after the resurrection became the basis for their expectation.

— The Genesee Diary

Often you will feel that nothing happens in your prayer. You say: "I am just sitting there and getting distracted." But if you develop the discipline of spending one half-hour a day listening to the voice of love, you will gradually discover that something is happening of which you were not even conscious. It might be only in retrospect that you discover the voice that blesses you. You thought that what happened during your time of listening was nothing more than a lot of confusion, but then you discover yourself looking forward to your quiet time and missing it when you can't have it. The movement of God's Spirit is very gentle, very soft — and hidden. It does not seek attention. But that movement is also very persistent, strong, and deep. It changes our hearts radically.

— Life of the Beloved

The Absence and Presence of God

In prayer, God's presence is never separated from God's absence and God's absence is never separated from God's presence. The presence of God is so much beyond the human experience of being together that it quite easily is perceived as absence. The absence of God, on the other hand, is often so deeply felt that it leads to a new sense of God's presence. This is powerfully expressed in Psalm 22:1–5:

> My God, my God, why have you deserted me?
> How far from saving me, the words I groan!
> I call all day, my God, but you never answer,
> all night long I call and cannot rest.
>
> Yet, Holy One, you
> who make your home in the praises of Israel,
> in you our fathers put their trust,
> they trusted and you rescued them;
> they called to you for help and they were saved,
> they never trusted you in vain.

This prayer not only is the expression of the experience of the people of Israel, but also the culmination of the Christian experience. When Jesus spoke these words on the cross, total aloneness and full acceptance touched each other. In that moment of complete emptiness all was fulfilled. In that hour of darkness new light was seen. While death was witnessed, life was affirmed. Where God's absence was most loudly expressed, God's presence was most profoundly revealed. . . . It is into this mystery that we enter when we pray.

— *Reaching Out*

Thirteen

Eucharist

Prayer finds its most profound expression in the breaking of the bread.
— Compassion

The Eucharist is the most ordinary and the most divine gesture imaginable.
— With Burning Hearts

Faithful to the Breaking of the Bread

As a discipline for living the moment fully and recognizing in it the healing presence of the Holy Spirit, prayer finds its most profound expression in the breaking of the bread. The intimate connection between compassion, prayer, and the breaking of the bread is made clear in the description of the early Christian community: "These remained faithful to the teaching of the apostles, to the brotherhood, to the breaking of bread.... They shared their food gladly and generously; they praised God and were looked up to by everyone" (Acts 2:42–47). The breaking of the bread stands at the center of the Christian community.... It is in the breaking of the bread together that the Holy Spirit, the Spirit sent by Christ and the Father, becomes most tangibly present to the community. The breaking of the bread, therefore, is not a moment in which we try to forget the pains of "real life" and withdraw into a dreamlike ceremony, but the festive articulation of what we perceive as the center of our lives.

When we break bread together, we reveal to each other the real story of Christ's life and our lives in him. Jesus took bread, blessed it, broke it, and gave it to his friends. He did so when he saw a hungry crowd and felt compassion for them (Matt. 14:19, 15:36); he did it on the evening before his death when he wanted to say farewell (Matt. 26:26); he did so when he made himself known to the two disciples whom he met on the road to Emmaus (Luke 24:30). And ever since his death, Christians have done so in memory of him. Thus, the breaking of the bread is the celebration, the making present, of Christ's story as well as our own. In the taking, blessing, breaking, and giving of the bread, the mystery of Christ's life is expressed in the most succinct way....

It is in this life that is taken, blessed, broken, and given that Jesus Christ wants to make us participants. Therefore, while breaking bread with his disciples, he said, "Do this as a memorial of me" (Luke 22:19). When we eat bread and drink wine together in memory of Christ, we become intimately related to his own compassionate life. In fact, we *become* his life and are thus enabled to re-present his life in our time and place. Our compassion becomes a manifestation of God's compassion lived out through all times and in all places.

— *Compassion*

"Bread Connections"

In the breaking of the bread together, we reclaim our own broken condition rather than denying its reality. We become more aware than ever that we are taken, set apart as witnesses for God; that we are blessed by words and acts of grace; and that we are broken, not in revenge or cruelty, but in order to become bread which can be given as food to others. When two, three, ten, a hundred, or a thousand people eat the same bread and drink from the same cup, and so become united with the broken and poured-out life of Christ, they discover that their own lives are part of that one life and thus recognize each other as brothers and sisters.

There are very few places left in our world where our common humanity can be lifted up and celebrated, but each time we come together around the simple signs of bread and wine, we tear down many walls and gain an inkling of God's intentions for the human family. And each time this happens we are called to become more concerned not only about each other's well-being but also about the well-being of all people in our world.

Thus, the breaking of the bread... brings us into contact with people whose bodies and minds have been broken by oppression and torture and whose lives are being destroyed in the prisons of this world. It brings us into touch with men, women, and children whose physical, mental, and spiritual beauty remains invisible due to lack of food and shelter....

These connections are indeed "bread connections" which challenge us to work with all our energy for the daily bread of all people. In this way our praying together becomes working together, and the call to break the same bread becomes a call to action. — *Compassion*

Jesus: Hidden in the Bread

I still remember Mother Teresa once saying to me that you can't see Jesus in the poor unless you can see him in the Eucharist. At the time, that remark seemed to me a bit high-flying and pious, but now that I've spent a year living with handicapped people, I'm beginning to understand better what she meant. It isn't really possible to see Jesus in human beings if you can't see him in the hidden reality of the bread that comes down from heaven. In human beings you can see this, that, and the other: angels and devils, saints and brutes, benevolent souls and malevolent power-maniacs. However, it's only when you've learned from personal experience how much Jesus cares for you and how much he desires to be your daily food, that you can learn to see that every human heart is a dwelling place for Jesus. When your heart is touched by the presence of Jesus in the Eucharist, then you will receive new eyes capable of recognizing that same presence in the hearts of others. Heart speaks to heart. Jesus in our heart speaks to Jesus in the hearts of our fellow men and women. That's the eucharistic mystery of which we are a part.

—*Letters to Marc about Jesus*

Participating in Jesus' Descending Way

The Eucharist is the sacrament of love, given to us as the means of finding that descending way of Jesus in our hearts. Jesus himself says, "I am the living bread which has come down from heaven. Anyone who eats this bread will live forever." You see here how the descending way of Jesus can become your way too. Whenever you eat the bread of heaven you not only become more profoundly united with Jesus, but you also learn gradually to walk his descending way with him.

Jesus wants to give himself to us so much that he has become food for us, and whenever we eat this food the longing is aroused in us also to give ourselves away to others. The self-surrendering love which we encounter in the Eucharist is the source of true Christian community. Paul makes that very clear when he presents the descending way of Jesus to us as the model for living in community. He says, "Make my joy complete by being of a single mind, one in love, one in heart and one in mind. Nothing is to be done out of jealousy or vanity; instead, out of humility of mind everyone should give preference to others, everyone pursuing not selfish interests but those of others."

This mind-set gives concrete form to the descending way of Jesus, who "did not count equality with God something to be grasped. But he emptied himself, taking the form of a slave." This is the eucharistic mind. Whenever we eat the body of Jesus and drink his blood, we participate in his descending way and so become a community in which competitiveness and rivalry have made way for the love of God.

If you yourself are seriously searching for the specific way which you must walk to follow Jesus, then I beg you not to do so on your own, but within a eucharistic community. I feel more and more certain that the way of Jesus can't be found outside the community of those who believe in Jesus and make their belief visible by coming together around the eucharistic table. The Eucharist is the heart and center of being-the-church. Without it there is no people of God, no community of faith, no church. Often enough, you see that people who abandon the church have trouble in holding on to Jesus. This becomes understandable when you consider that the church is the eucharistic community in which Jesus gives us his body and blood as gifts that come to us from heaven and help us to find the way of love in our own lives.

— Letters to Marc about Jesus

Entering into Communion

Every time we invite Jesus into our homes, that is to say, into our life with all its light and dark sides, and offer him the place of honor at our table, he takes the bread and the cup and hands them to us saying: "Take and eat, this is my body. Take and drink, this is my blood. Do this to remember me. . . . "

The Eucharist is the most ordinary and the most divine gesture imaginable. That is the truth of Jesus. So human, yet so divine; so familiar, yet so mysterious; so close, yet so revealing! But that is the story of Jesus who "being in the form of God did not count equality with God something to be grasped, but emptied himself, taking the form of a slave, becoming as human beings are; and being in every way like a human being, he was humbler yet, even to accepting death, death on a cross" (Phil. 2:18). It is the story of God who wants to come close to us, so close that we can see God with our own eyes, hear God with our own ears, touch God with our own hands; so close that there is nothing between us and God, nothing that separates, nothing that divides, nothing that creates distance.

Jesus is God-for-us, God-with-us, God-within-us. Jesus is God giving himself completely, pouring himself out for us without reserve. Jesus doesn't hold back or cling to his own possessions. He gives all there is to give. "Eat, drink, this is my body, this is my blood ... this is me for you!"

•

It is this intense desire of God to enter into the most intimate relationship with us that forms the core of the eucharistic celebration and the eucharistic life. God not only wants to enter human history by becoming a person who lives in a specific epoch and a specific country, but God wants to become our daily food and drink at any time and any place. ...

Communion is what God wants and what we want. It is the deepest cry of God's and our heart, because we are made with a heart that can be satisfied only by the One who made it. God created in our heart a yearning for communion that no one but God can, and wants, to fulfill. God knows this. We seldom do. We keep looking somewhere else for that experience of belonging. ... Still if we have mourned our losses, listened to him on the road, and invited him into our innermost being, we will know that the communion we have been waiting to receive is the same communion God has been waiting to give.   — *With Burning Hearts*

Becoming Christ

Communion with Jesus means becoming like him. With him we are nailed on the cross, with him we are laid in the tomb, with him we are raised up to accompany lost travelers on their journey. Communion, becoming Christ, leads us to a new realm of being. It ushers us into the Kingdom. There the old distinctions between happiness and sadness, success and failure, praise and blame, health and sickness, life and death, no longer exist. There we no longer belong to the world that keeps dividing, judging, separating, and evaluating. There we belong to Christ and Christ to us, and with Christ we belong to God. Suddenly the two disciples, who ate the bread and recognized him, are alone again. But not with the aloneness with which they began their journey. They are alone, together, and know that a new bond has been created between them. They no longer look at the ground with downcast faces. They look at each other and say: "Did our hearts not burn when he talked to us on the road and explained the Scriptures to us?"   — *With Burning Hearts*

The Eucharistic Life

Eucharist — thanksgiving — in the end, comes from above. It is the gift that we cannot fabricate for ourselves. It is to be received. It is freely offered and asks to be freely received. That is where the choice is! We can choose to let the stranger continue his journey and so remain a stranger. But we can also invite him into our inner lives, let him touch every part of our being and then transform our resentments into gratitude. We don't have to do this. In fact, most people don't. But as often as we make that choice, everything, even the most trivial things, become new. Our little lives become great — part of the mysterious work of God's salvation. Once that happens, nothing is accidental, casual, or futile any more. Even the most insignificant event speaks the language of faith, hope, and, above all, love. That's the eucharistic life, the life in which everything becomes a way of saying "Thank you" to the One who joined us on the road.

— With Burning Hearts

Fourteen

Death and Eternal Life

Death is not the end but the beginning.

— The Road to Peace

Jesus says: "Dwell in me as I dwell in you." It is this divine in-dwelling that is eternal life.

— Here and Now

The Heavenly Prize

Do we have a clear goal in life? ... Without a clear goal, we
will always be distracted and spend our energy on secondary
things. "Keep your eye on the prize," Martin Luther King said
to his people. What is our prize? It is the divine life, the
eternal life, the life with and in God. Jesus proclaimed to us
that goal, that heavenly prize. To Nicodemus he said: "This is
how God loved the world: he gave his Son so that everyone
who believes in him may not perish but may have eternal
life" (John 3:16).

It is not easy to keep our eyes fixed on the eternal life, especially not in a world that keeps telling us that there are
more immediate and urgent things on which to focus. ...
How then do we keep our goal clear, how then do we fix
our eyes on the prize? By the discipline of prayer; the discipline that helps us to bring God back again and again to
the center of our life. We will always remain distracted, constantly busy with many urgent demands, but when there is a
time and place set apart to return to our God who offers us
eternal life, we gradually can come to realize that the many
things we have to do, to say, or to think no longer distract
us but are, instead, all leading us closer to our goal. Most important, however, is that our goal remains clear. Prayer keeps
our goal clear, and when our goal has become vague, prayer
makes it clear again.   — *Here and Now*

When Is Eternal Life?

Eternal life. Where is it? When is it? For a long time I have
thought about eternal life as a life after all my birthdays have

run out. For most of my years I have spoken about the eternal life as the "afterlife," as "life after death." But the older I become, the less interest my "afterlife" holds for me. Worrying not only about tomorrow, next year, and the next decade, but even about the next life seems a false preoccupation. Wondering how things will be for me after I die seems, for the most part, a distraction. When my clear goal is the eternal life, that life must be reachable right now, where I am, because eternal life is life in and with God, and God is where I am here and now.

The great mystery of the spiritual life — the life in God — is that we don't have to wait for it as something that will happen later. Jesus says: "Dwell in me as I dwell in you." It is this divine in-dwelling that is eternal life. It is the active presence of God at the center of my living — the movement of God's Spirit within us — that gives us the eternal life.

But still, what about life after death? When we live in communion with God, when we belong to God's own household, there is no longer any "before" or "after." Death is no longer the dividing line. Death has lost its power over those who belong to God, because God is the God of the living, not of the dead. Once we have tasted the joy and peace that come from being embraced by God's love, we know that all is well and will be well. "Don't be afraid," Jesus says. "I have overcome the powers of death... come and dwell with me and know that where I am your God is."

When eternal life is our clear goal, it is not a distant goal. It is a goal that can be reached in the present moment. When our heart understands this divine truth, we are living the spiritual life.

•

The great spiritual challenge is to discover, over time, that the limited, conditional, and temporal love we receive from parents, husbands, wives, children, teachers, colleagues, and friends is a reflection of the unlimited, unconditional, and everlasting love of God. Whenever we can make that huge leap of faith we will know that death is no longer the end but the gateway to the fullness of the Divine Love.

— Here and Now

Nurturing the Eternal Life within Us

The knowledge that Jesus came to dress our mortal bodies with immortality must help us develop an inner desire to be born to a new, eternal life with him and encourage us to find ways to prepare for it.

It is important to nurture constantly the life of the Spirit of Jesus — which is the eternal life — that is already in us. Baptism gave us this life, the Eucharist maintains it, and our many spiritual practices — such as prayer, meditation, spiritual reading, and spiritual guidance — can help us to deepen and solidify it. The sacramental life and life with the Word of God gradually make us ready to let go of our mortal bodies and receive the mantle of immortality. Thus death is not the enemy who puts an end to everything but the friend who takes us by the hand and leads us into the Kingdom of eternal love.   *— Bread for the Journey*

Befriending Our Death

It seems indeed important that we face death before we are in any real danger of dying and reflect on our mortality before all conscious and unconscious energy is directed to the struggle to survive. It is important to be prepared for death, very important; but if we start thinking about it only when we are terminally ill, our reflections will not give us the support we need. . . .

I think, then, that our first task is to befriend death. I like that expression "to befriend." I first heard it used by a Jungian analyst James Hillman when he attended a seminar I taught on Christian Spirituality at Yale Divinity School. . . . He emphasized the importance of "befriending": befriending your dreams, befriending your shadow, befriending your unconscious. He made it convincingly clear that in order to become full human beings, we have to claim the totality of our experience; we come to maturity by integrating not only the light but also the dark side of our stories into our selfhood. . . .

And isn't death, the frightening unknown that lurks in the depths of our unconscious minds, like a great shadow that we perceive only dimly in our dreams? Befriending death seems to be the basis of all other forms of befriending. I have a deep sense, hard to articulate, that if we could really befriend death, we would be free people. So many of our doubts and hesitations, ambivalences and insecurities, are bound up with our deep-seated fear of death, that our lives would be significantly different if we could relate to death as a familiar guest instead of a threatening stranger.

But how do we befriend death? . . . I think love — deep, human love — does not know death. . . . Real love says,

"Forever." Love will always reach out toward the eternal. Love comes from that place within us where death cannot enter. Love does not accept the limits of hours, days, weeks, months, years, or centuries. Love is not willing to be imprisoned by time....

The same love that reveals the absurdity of death also allows us to befriend death. The same love that forms the basis of our grief is also the basis of our hope; the same love that makes us cry out in pain also must enable us to develop a liberating intimacy with our own most basic brokenness. Without faith, this must sound like a contradiction. But our faith in Jesus, whose love overcame death and who rose from the grave on the third day, converts this contradiction into a paradox, the most healing paradox of our existence.

— A Letter of Consolation

The Resurrection

The resurrection does not solve our problems about dying and death. It is not the happy ending to our life's struggle, nor is it the big surprise that God has kept in store for us. No, the resurrection is the expression of God's faithfulness to Jesus and to all God's children. Through the resurrection, God has said to Jesus, "You are indeed my beloved Son, and my love is everlasting," and to us God has said, "You indeed are my beloved children, and my love is everlasting." The resurrection is God's way of revealing to us that nothing that belongs to God will ever go to waste. What belongs to God will never get lost — not even our mortal bodies. The resurrection doesn't answer any of our curious questions about life after death, such as, How will it be? How will it look? But it does reveal to us that, indeed, love is stronger than death. After that revelation, we must remain silent, leave the whys, wheres, hows, and whens behind, and simply trust.

— *Our Greatest Gift*

Living in the House of Love

Through Christ's victory over all death, individual as well as collective, death has no final power over us any longer. We are no longer locked in the dark world of despair but have already found our home in God where death has no place and life is everlasting. Though we are still in this world, we no longer belong to it. Our faith allows us even now to be members of God's household, and taste even now the inexhaustible love of God. It is this knowledge of where we truly belong that sets us free to be fierce resisters against death while humbly, compassionately, and joyfully proclaiming life wherever we go. — *The Road to Peace*

Coming Home to Jesus

Somewhere, deep in me, I sensed that my life was in real danger. And so I let myself enter into a place I had never been before: the portal of death. I wanted to know that place, to "walk around" it, and make myself ready for a life beyond life. It was the first time in my life that I consciously walked into this seemingly fearful place, the first time I looked forward to what might be a new way of being. I tried to let go of my familiar world...I tried not to look back, but ahead.

I kept looking at that door that might open to me and show me something beyond anything I had ever seen.

•

I knew very concretely that he was there for me, but also that he was embracing the universe. I knew that, indeed, he was the Jesus I had prayed to and spoken about, but also that now he did not ask for prayers or words. All was well. The words that summarize it all are "Life" and "Love." But these words were incarnate in a real presence. Death lost its power and shrank away in the Life and Love that surrounded me in such an intimate way, as if I were walking through a sea whose waves were rolled away. I was being held safe while moving toward the other shore. All jealousies, resentments, and angers were being gently moved away, and I was being shown that Love and Life are greater, deeper, and stronger than any of the forces I had been worrying about.

One emotion was very strong — that of homecoming. Jesus opened his home to me and seemed to say, "Here is where you belong." The words he spoke to his disciples, "In my Father's house there are many places to live in....I am going now to prepare a place for you" (John 14:2), became very real. The risen Jesus, who now dwells with his Father, was welcoming me home after a long journey.

This experience was the realization of my oldest and deepest desires. Since the first moment of consciousness, I have had the desire to be with Jesus. Now I felt his presence in a most tangible way, as if my whole life had come together and I was being enfolded in love. The homecoming had a real quality of return, a return to the womb of God.

•

As I felt life weakening in me, I felt a deep desire to forgive and to be forgiven, to let go of all evaluations and
opinions, to be free from the burden of judgments. I said
to Sue, "Please tell everyone who has hurt me that I forgive them from my heart, and please ask everyone whom
I have hurt to forgive me too." As I said this, I felt I was
taking off the wide leather belts that I had worn while chap-
lain with the rank of captain in the army. Those belts not
only girded my waist, but also crossed my chest and shoulders. They had given me prestige and power. They had
encouraged me to judge people and put them in their place.
Although my stay in the army was very brief, I had, in my
mind, never fully removed my belts. But I knew now that
I did not want to die with these belts holding me captive.
I had to die powerless, without belts, completely free from
judgment.

•

From that moment on I gave myself over to Jesus and felt like
a little chick safe under the wings of its mother. That sense
of safety had something to do with the consciousness that
anguish had come to an end: anguish from not being able to
receive the love I wanted to receive, and from not being able
to give the love I most wanted to give; anguish caused by
feelings of rejection and abandonment. The blood that I was
losing in such quantity became a metaphor for the anguish
that had plagued me for so many years. It too would flow
out of me, and I would come to know the love that I had
yearned for with all my heart. Jesus was there to offer me the
love of his Father, a love that I most desired to receive, a love
also that would enable me to give all. Jesus himself had lived
anguish. He knew the pain of being unable to give or receive

what he most valued. But he lived through that anguish with the trust that his Father, who had sent him, would never leave him alone. And now Jesus was there, standing beyond all anguish and calling me to "the other country."

—*Beyond the Mirror*

A Sacred Moment

Everything was truthful, there was no lie. Mother was dying and nobody denied it. Although her suffering was deep and mysterious, it was not hidden from us. We experienced the privilege of being close to her suffering, intimately connected with her pain, deeply united with her agony....I have never felt so strongly that the truth can make us free. It was a very sacred moment, and I was blessed to be there....

As the long hours passed into longer nights and days, [Mother's] cry became deeper and stronger. Bending over her, I heard her words of prayer: "My Father who art in heaven, I believe, I hope, I love....My God, my Father...." I knew that this was the struggle of the great encounter. I wanted to give her the freedom she needed to enter into this lonely hour, to give her the space where this most mysterious of events could take place. I knew that she needed more than comforting words; she needed whatever support we could give her in this struggle of faith. With my father, brothers, and sister, I prayed the prayers she hinted at....In this way, we felt as if we offered her the words she could no longer speak herself, surrounding her with a shield of prayer that allowed her to fight her lonely battle.   —*In Memoriam*

Fruitfulness and Death

I want to leave with you, in the end, that very deep word that Jesus says about death: "It is for your good that I'm going, because unless I go I cannot send you my Spirit." That word has to be rediscovered. Jesus, who died in his early thirties and who spoke about his death from the very beginning of his proclamation, is saying that his death is not the end but the beginning. It is not something to be afraid of, but something that opens a whole new world. Death is the place that allows him to send his love, his Spirit, his deepest self. And somehow, preparing ourselves for our death, helping others prepare themselves for theirs, means that we realize that our spirits and theirs will touch generations yet to come. Yes, we have to die with Christ, but we will be raised with Christ so as to send the Spirit of Christ.

This morning's reading was from the book of Sirach, about those whom we have buried but who are here with us, continuing to send us their wisdom so we can live. Do we really believe that? It means that I will be around for generations because I keep sending my spirit, my spirit which is from God and isn't going to die. In fact, that spirit was given to me, not just for these thirty or fifty or seventy years, but so that it can bear fruit long after my life on earth is over. It is precisely my vulnerability, my brokenness, and my death which allow me to be fruitful. "Fruitful," not "successful." And therefore, the main question is not "How much can I still do?" although that's not unimportant. The main question is, "How can I make my life fruitful? How can my dying be not the end of fruitfulness but rather its fullest realization?" Jesus lived that way, and we are called to live that way too. Then we may be able, gently, to let people who are dying discover that they are going to bear fruit far into the future, beyond their lifetimes. I think that's good news, really good news!

— *The Road to Peace*

Ecstatic Living

Jesus said, "Live ecstatically. Move out of that place of death and toward life because I am the God who is living. Wherever I am, there is life, there is change, there is growth, there is increase and blossoming and something new. I am going to make everything new."

For us to dare to live a life in which we continue to move out of the static places and take trusting steps in new directions — that is what faith is about. The Greek word for faith means to trust — to trust that the ground before you that you never walked on is safe ground, God's ground, holy ground.

Walk and don't be afraid. Don't want to have it all charted out for you. Let it happen. Let something new grow. That is the walk of faith — walking with the Lord, always walking away from the familiar places. "Leave your father, leave your mother, leave your brother, leave your sister. Follow me. I am the Lord of love." And wherever there is love, fear will be wiped out. "Perfect love casts out all fear."

You can go out and you will live. You will live eternally because Jesus is the Lord of life. That is the ecstasy. You can start participating in it every time you step out of your fear and out of the sameness. It doesn't require big jumps, but simply small steps.

Do you choose life? Or are you choosing death, that fearful place where you hang on to what you are most familiar with? Ecstatic living, real joy, is precisely connected with stepping onto unknown ground, trusting that you are in safe hands. — "Intimacy, Fecundity and Ecstasy"

Trusting in the Catcher

All true care for the dying person brings new awareness of the bonds that create a community of love.

The Flying Rodleighs are trapeze artists who perform in the German circus Simoneit-Barum. When the circus came to Freiburg two years ago, my friends Franz and Reny invited me and my father to see the show. I will never forget how enraptured I became when I first saw the Rodleighs move through the air, flying and catching as elegant dancers. The next day, I returned to the circus to see them again and introduced myself to them as one of their great fans. They invited me to attend their practice sessions, gave me free tickets, asked me to dinner, and suggested I travel with them for a week in the near future. I did, and we became good friends.

One day, I was sitting with Rodleigh, the leader of the troupe, in his caravan, talking about flying. He said, "As a flyer, I must have complete trust in my catcher. The public might think that I am the great star of the trapeze, but the real star is Joe, my catcher. He has to be there for me with split-second precision and grab me out of the air as I come to him in the long jump." "How does it work?" I asked. "The secret," Rodleigh said, "is that the flyer does nothing and the catcher does everything. When I fly to Joe, I have simply to stretch out my arms and hands and wait for him to catch me and pull me safely over the apron behind the catchbar."

"You do nothing!" I said, surprised. "Nothing," Rodleigh repeated. "The worst thing the flyer can do is to try to catch the catcher. I am not supposed to catch Joe. It's Joe's task to catch me. If I grabbed Joe's wrists, I might break them, or he might break mine, and that would be the end for both of us. A flyer must fly, and a catcher must catch, and the flyer must trust, with outstretched arms, that his catcher will be there for him."

When Rodleigh said this with so much conviction, the words of Jesus flashed through my mind: "Father, into your hands I commend my Spirit." Dying is trusting in the catcher. To care for the dying is to say, "Don't be afraid. Remember that you are the beloved child of God. He will be there when you make your long jump. Don't try to grab him; he will grab you. Just stretch out your arms and hands and trust, trust, trust."
                                                                    —*Our Greatest Gift*

Fifteen

Prayers

*It is my hope, therefore, that those who recognize
in these prayers the cries of their own hearts will
also recognize the quiet prayer of God's Spirit in
the midst of their own halting and stuttering words.*

—A Cry for Mercy

*Let me keep saying with my heart as well as my
lips, "I love you, Lord, with my whole heart, soul,
and mind."*

—Unpublished manuscript

Dear Lord, give me a growing desire to pray. It remains so hard for me to give my time generously to you. I am still greedy for time — time to be useful, effective, successful, time to perform, excel, produce. But you, O Lord, ask nothing else than my simple presence, my humble recognition of my nakedness, my defenseless confession of my sins, so that you can let the rays of your love enter my heart and give me the deep knowledge that I can love because you have loved me first, that I can offer acceptance because you have accepted me first, and that I can do good because you have shown me your goodness first.

What holds me back? What makes me so hesitant and stingy, so careful and calculating? Do I still doubt that I need nothing besides you? Do I still want to build up some kind of reserve in case you might not come through? Please, Lord, help me to give up these immature games, and let me love you freely, boldly, courageously, and generously. Amen.

—A Cry for Mercy

O Lord, who else or what else can I desire but you? You are my Lord, Lord of my heart, mind, and soul. You know me through and through. In and through you everything that is finds its origin and goal. You embrace all that exists and care for it with divine love and compassion. Why, then, do I keep expecting happiness and satisfaction outside of you? Why do I keep relating to you as one of my many relationships, instead of my only relationship, in which all other ones are grounded? Why do I keep looking for popularity, respect from others, success, acclaim, and sensual pleasures? Why, Lord, is it so hard for me to make you the only one? Why do I keep hesitating to surrender myself totally to you?

Help me, O Lord, to let my old self die, to let die the thousand big and small ways in which I am still building up my false self and trying to cling to my false desires. Let me be reborn in you and see through you the world in the right way, so that all my actions, words, and thoughts can become a hymn of praise to you.

I need your loving grace to travel on this hard road that leads to the death of my old self and to a new life in and for you. I know and trust that this is the road to freedom. Lord, dispel my mistrust and help me become a trusting friend. Amen. — *A Cry for Mercy*

O Lord Jesus, your words to your Father were born out of your silence. Lead me into this silence, so that my words may be spoken in your name and thus be fruitful. It is so hard to be silent, silent with my mouth, but even more, silent with my heart. There is so much talking going on within me. It seems that I am always involved in inner debates with myself, my friends, my enemies, my supporters, my opponents, my colleagues, and my rivals. But this inner debate reveals how far my heart is from you. If I were simply to rest at your feet and realize that I belong to you and you alone, I would easily stop arguing with all the real and imagined people around me. These arguments show my insecurity, my fear, my apprehensions, and my need for being recognized and receiving attention. You, O Lord, will give me all the attention I need if I would simply stop talking and start listening to you. I know that in the silence of my heart you will speak to me and show me your love. Give me, O Lord, that silence. Let me be patient and grow slowly into this silence in which I can be with you. Amen. — *A Cry for Mercy*

Dear Lord, your loving friend Francis de Sales tells me to let
my life be guided by love. Love of you, not fear of you. I know
that many writers stress the importance of fear in my relationship to you. You are my judge, you know me through and
through, nothing is hidden from you. You see me deeper and
more accurately than I can see myself. All that inspires me
with fear and awe, but it also tends to paralyze me and keep
me away from you. I pray that my love may be stronger than
my fear, and that I will run to you always, notwithstanding
my sins, imperfections, double motives, and many impurities.
Let me always realize that you gave yourself for me and for all
people out of love, and that the only thing you want is my
love — my free, open, spontaneous, and generous love. Let
me keep saying with my heart as well as my lips, "I love you,
Lord, with my whole heart, soul, and mind." I want to make
that love be the guide in my relationship with you. Amen.

—Unpublished manuscript

Dear Lord, your name is "of all names in the world, the only
one by which we can be saved." I pray that I may imprint
your name on my heart, that your name will give meaning
and power to all that I think, say, or do, and that your name
will be the center to which and from which all my attention
moves. I pray that your name will so fully pervade my being
that one day you will recognize yourself in me and then call
me to your home.

I still feel so far from the realization of this desire. But
at least I have a clear goal. Be my shepherd, and guide me
on my way to you. Be a gentle, loving, caring shepherd who
wants to keep me close to you. Let a mutual knowing grow
between you and me, a knowing by which not only you know
me but I also come to know you. It is this mutual knowl-

edge that will make me desire to live more and more in your name and to let your name save me from my sins, my false bonds, my inner darkness, and my final death. Stay with me always. Amen. —Unpublished manuscript

Dear Lord, in the midst of much inner turmoil and restlessness, there is a consoling thought: maybe you are working in me in a way I cannot yet feel, experience, or understand. My mind is not able to concentrate on you, my heart is not able to remain centered, and it seems as if you are absent and have left me alone. But in faith I cling to you. I believe that your Spirit reaches deeper and further than my mind or heart, and that profound movements are not the first to be noticed.

Therefore, Lord, I promise I will not run away, not give up, not stop praying, even when it all seems useless, pointless, and a waste of time and effort. I want to let you know that I love you even though I do not feel loved by you, and that I hope in you even though I often experience despair. Let this be a little dying I can do with you and for you as a way of experiencing some solidarity with the millions in this world who suffer far more than I do. Amen. —A Cry for Mercy

Dear Lord, you said to your disciples: "All I have learned from my Father, I have made known to you." That is the intimacy to which you invite those who believe in you. You do not want to hide anything from us. You want to give us all you have, all you are. It is impossible for me to grasp the immense, boundless mystery of your love and goodness. You indeed want me to be as close to your heavenly Father as you are. You want me to know what you know, to hear what you hear, and to see what you see. You want me to become a son of God as you are a Son of God. Is there anything else I can desire? O Lord, who am I that you invite me to this friendship? Who am I that you want to reveal to me your own most intimate life and, more wonderful still, that you want me to become part of it?

Why, then, do I keep desiring other things, when you want to give me all? Please, Lord, open my heart and mind to become more aware of this profound mystery of your love. I am a broken sinner, so sinful that I am blind and deaf to your divine invitation. Make me see and hear, and keep forgiving me my stubbornness and lack of faith. I believe, Lord; help my unbelief. Amen.   — Unpublished manuscript

Dear Lord, in your heart no malice can be found. Your heart does not know resentment, hatred, suspicion, or rivalry. Your heart knows only love, love without limitation, without reservation, without condition. Your heart speaks of gentleness, tenderness, forgiveness, joy, peace, and freedom. Your heart is open to all who want to come, whatever their burden is. You say: "Come to me, all you who labor and are overburdened, and I will give you rest. Learn from me, for I am gentle and humble of heart."

I pray to you, O Lord, that I may always enter deeper into the mystery of your sacred heart and there find the source of all consolation and comfort. May I become so fully immersed in the love that comes forth from your heart that I cannot be anything other than a living witness of your boundless love to all whom I meet. Amen.   — Unpublished manuscript

Dear Lord, I love you. You are all I desire, all I hope for, all I long for. You are beautiful, good, kind, gentle, just, peaceful, forgiving, merciful, and loving. To you I direct my eyes; to you I stretch out my arms; to you I lift up my heart. You are my Lord and my God.

I know, Lord, that I think about many things which keep my mind from you, look at many things which do not lead me to you, and do many things which do not bring me closer to you. I know that on the surface I am restless and distracted. But I also know that the center of my being cries out to you, even though this cry has not yet permeated all my senses.

Accept, O Lord, my love, even when my ears and eyes, my lips and hands are not fully disciplined yet in the service of love. Accept my love as a desire to love you more every day. Amen. —Unpublished manuscript

O Lord, how often I desire signs and wonders in order to be strengthened in my faith! I want you to appear to me as you did to Paul on the road to Damascus, or to give me a sudden inner sense of your presence which blots out all my doubts and hesitations. But you said that it was lack of faith that prevented you from being known. You couldn't work many miracles in Nazareth because your countrymen could only see in you a carpenter's son.

O Lord, deepen and strengthen my faith so that I can see with new eyes and hear with new ears the signs and signals of your presence in my own world. It is my blindness and deafness which keeps me from being fully aware of your powerful actions here and now. You are present; you work wonders no less today than in the days of your life with your disciples.

Then, just as now, some saw and some remained blind, some heard and some remained deaf. Most people "knew" you too well to come to truly know you.

Let me recognize you, and let me say with all my mind, heart, and soul, "You are the Christ, the Son of the living God." Amen.   —Unpublished manuscript

O Lord, you are the Word, spoken from eternity by the Father. You came to dwell among us and to lead us with you to your Father's house.

You are the Son, born from eternity of the Father. You were born among us to make us your brothers and sisters, sons and daughters of your Father.

You are the Light, shining forth from eternity from the God of Light. You entered into our darkness to enlighten us with divine light.

You are the Life, coming forth from the living God from all ages. You experienced death with us and thus opened to us the way of eternal life.

You are the Truth, true Son from true God. You suffered in a world full of lies and illusions and so revealed to us the joy of the true knowledge of God.

I thank you. I praise you. I worship you. Amen.
                                        —Unpublished manuscript

Dear Lord, give me eyes to see and ears to hear. I know there is a light in the darkness that makes everything new. I know there is new life in suffering that opens a new earth to me. I know there is joy beyond sorrow that rejuvenates my heart. Yes, Lord, I know that you are, that you act, that you love, that you indeed are Light, Life, and Truth. People, work, plans, projects, ideas, meetings, buildings, paintings, music, and literature all can only give me real joy and peace when I can see and hear them as reflections of your presence, your glory, your kingdom.

Let me then see and hear. Let me be so taken by what you show me and by what you say to me that your vision and hearing become my guide in life and impart meaning to all my concerns.

Let me see and hear what is really real, and let me have the courage to keep unmasking endless unrealities, which disturb my life every day. Now I see only in a mirror, but one day, O Lord, I hope to see you face to face. Amen.

— Unpublished manuscript

Dear Lord, how often have the worries of the world and the attraction of wealth choked your word! For your word to grow deep roots and to yield a rich harvest, it needs a free, open, and untroubled heart. I know, Lord, that your word has power, that it can transform heart and mind and can become so strong that it speaks as if by itself. But how can your word be effective when it is received by a thorny heart, a heart constantly and scrupulously reflecting on what happened yesterday and anxiously anticipating what will happen tomorrow, a heart perverted by guilt, jealousy, envy, and lust, a heart always restless and in turmoil? It is no surprise that such a heart prevents your word from bearing fruit.

O Lord, give me a heart that can receive your word the way good soil receives the falling seed, and let your word produce new life and new love in the midst of this barren world. Amen.
— *A Cry for Mercy*

Dear Lord, today I have been thinking about the mustard seed. You compare the kingdom of God to this smallest of all seeds, and point to its potential to grow into the biggest shrub of all that can give shelter to many birds.

Underneath all the events and activities of the day, which often seem so distracting and confusing, the little seed is hidden which you have planted. I am so impatient. I want so much to see the big shrub from the very start. But why? You are a patient Lord. You let your kingdom grow in me with the same imperceptibility but also with the same power as the mustard seed. You allow your presence to remain hidden very long.

I know, Lord, that you want me to be faithful, to hold on to the knowledge that the seed is growing even when I do not see or feel it, and to move through life with the deep conviction that one day I will see clearly that you never were absent but always were preparing me for the day when the seed you had planted would show its full presence. Help me to be faithful and patient as you are. Amen.

—Unpublished manuscript

Dear God,
I am so afraid to open my clenched fists!
Who will I be when I have nothing left to hold on to?
Who will I be when I stand before you with empty
    hands?
Please help me to gradually open my hands
and to discover that I am not what I own,
but what you want to give me.
And what you want to give me is love,
unconditional, everlasting love.
Amen.
                     —*With Open Hands*

Dear God,
Speak gently in my silence.
When the loud outer noises of my surroundings
and the loud inner noises of my fears
keep pulling me away from you,
help me to trust that you are still there
even when I am unable to hear you.
Give me ears to listen to your small, soft voice saying:
"Come to me, you who are overburdened,
and I will give you rest ...
for I am gentle and humble of heart."
Let that loving voice be my guide.
Amen.   — *With Open Hands*

Dear God,
I so much want to be in control.
I want to be the master of my own destiny.
Still I know that you are saying:
"Let me take you by the hand and lead you.
Accept my love
and trust that where I will bring you,
the deepest desires of your heart will be fulfilled."
Lord, open my hands to receive your gift of love.
Amen.   — *With Open Hands*

Dear God,
I am full of wishes,
full of desires,
full of expectations.
Some of them may be realized, many may not,

but in the midst
of all my satisfactions and disappointments,
I hope in you.
I know that you will never leave me alone
and will fulfill your divine promises.
Even when it seems that things are not going my way,
I know that they are going your way
and that in the end your way is the best way for me.
O Lord, strengthen my hope,
especially when my many wishes are not fulfilled.
Let me never forget that your name is Love.
Amen.   —*With Open Hands*

Dear God,
As you draw me ever deeper into your heart,
I discover that my companions on the journey
are women and men
loved by you as fully and as intimately as I am.
In your compassionate heart,
there is a place for all of them.
No one is excluded.
Give me a share in your compassion, dear God,
so that your unlimited love may become visible
in the way I love my brothers and sisters.
Amen.   —*With Open Hands*

An Advent Prayer

Dear Lord, help me keep my eyes on you. You are the incarnation of Divine Love, you are the expression of God's

infinite compassion, you are the visible manifestation of the Father's holiness. You are beauty, goodness, gentleness, forgiveness, and mercy. In you all can be found. Outside of you nothing can be found. Why should I look elsewhere or go elsewhere? You have the words of eternal life, you are food and drink, you are the Way, the Truth, and the Life. You are the light that shines in the darkness, the lamp on the lamp stand, the house on the hilltop. You are the perfect Icon of God. In and through you I can see the Heavenly Father, and with you I can find my way to him. O Holy One, Beautiful One, Glorious One, be my Lord, my Savior, my Redeemer, my Guide, my Consoler, my Comforter, my Hope, my Joy, and my Peace. To you I want to give all that I am. Let me be generous, not stingy or hesitant. Let me give you all — all I have, think, do and feel. It is yours, O Lord. Please accept it and make it fully your own. Amen.   —*A Cry for Mercy*

A Christmas Prayer

O Lord, how hard it is to accept your way. You come to me as a small, powerless child born away from home. You live for me as a stranger in your own land. You die for me as a criminal outside the walls of the city, rejected by your own people, misunderstood by your friends, and feeling abandoned by your God.

As I prepare to celebrate your birth, I am trying to feel loved, accepted, and at home in this world, and I am trying to overcome the feelings of alienation and separation which continue to assail me. But I wonder now if my deep sense of homelessness does not bring me closer to you than my occasional feelings of belonging. Where do I truly celebrate your birth: in a cozy home or in an unfamiliar house, among welcoming friends or among unknown strangers, with feelings of well-being or with feelings of loneliness?

I do not have to run away from those experiences that are closest to yours. Just as you do not belong to this world, so I do not belong to this world. Every time I feel this way I have an occasion to be grateful and to embrace you better and taste more fully your joy and peace.

Come, Lord Jesus, and be with me where I feel poorest. I trust that this is the place where you will find your manger and bring your light. Come, Lord Jesus, come.

Amen.   — *The Road to Daybreak*

A Prayer for the New Year

I am starting this year with the prayer of Charles de Fou-cauld, the prayer I say every day with much trepidation:

> Father, I abandon myself into your hands.
> Do with me whatever you will.
> Whatever you may do, I thank you.
> I am ready for all, I accept all.
> Let only your will be done in me,
> and in all your creatures.
>
> Into your hands I commend my spirit.
> I offer it to you with all the love that is in my heart.
> For I love you, Lord, and so want to give myself,
> to surrender myself into your hands,
> without reserve and with boundless confidence,
> for you are my Father.
> Amen.   — *Sabbatical Journey*

Lenten Prayers

Dear Lord Jesus,

Tomorrow the Lenten season begins. It is a time to be with you in a special way, a time to pray, to fast, and thus to follow you on your way to Jerusalem, to Golgotha, and to the final victory over death.

I am still so divided. I truly want to follow you, but I also want to follow my own desires and lend an ear to the voices that speak about prestige, success, human respect, pleasure, power, and influence. Help me to become deaf to these voices and more attentive to your voice, which calls me to choose the narrow road to life.

I know that Lent is going to be a very hard time for me. The choice for your way has to be made every moment of my life. I have to choose thoughts that are your thoughts, words that are your words, and actions that are your actions. There are no times or places without choices. And I know how deeply I resist choosing you.

Please, Lord, be with me at every moment and in every place. Give me the strength and the courage to live this season faithfully, so that, when Easter comes, I will be able to taste with joy the new life which you have prepared for me.

Amen.   — *The Road to Daybreak*

O Lord, it is a great grace that I can be in this monastery during Lent. How often have I lived through these weeks without paying much attention to penance, fasting, and prayer? How often have I missed the spiritual fruits of this season without even being aware of it? But how can I ever really celebrate Easter without observing Lent? How can I rejoice fully in your resurrection when I have avoided participating in your death?

Yes, Lord, I have to die — with you, through you, and in you — and thus become ready to recognize you when you appear to me in your resurrection. There is so much in me that needs to die: false attachments, greed and anger, impatience and stinginess. O Lord, I am self-centered, concerned about myself, my career, my future, my name and fame. Often I even feel that I use you for my own advantage. How preposterous, how sacrilegious, how sad! But yes, Lord, I know it is true. I know that often I have spoken about you, written about you, and acted in your name for my own glory and for my own success. Your name has not led me to persecution, oppression, or rejection. Your name has brought me rewards! I see clearly now how little I have died with you, really gone your way and been faithful to it. O Lord, make this Lenten season different from the other ones. Let me find you again. Amen.   —*A Cry for Mercy*

O Lord, my God and Savior, Jesus Christ, I keep asking you to give me the grace of conversion. Day and night I hope for only one thing: that you show your mercy to me and let me experience your presence in my heart. Let me come to a genuine act of repentance, to an honest humble prayer, and to a free spontaneous generosity. I see so clearly the road to follow! I understand so well what is necessary for me to come to you. I can speak and teach eloquently about life in you. But my heart hesitates, my inner and deepest self still holds back, wanting to bargain, wanting to say "Yes, but...."

O Lord, do I keep forgetting that you love me, that you are waiting for me with open arms? As a father with tears in his eyes, you see how your son is destroying the very life you gave him. Yet as a father you know, too, that you cannot force me to come back to you. Only when I freely come to you, when I freely shake off the false cares and troubles and freely confess my false ways and freely pray for mercy, only then can you freely give me your love.

Hear my prayer, O Lord, hear my plea, hear my desire to return to you. Do not leave me alone in my struggle. Save me from eternal damnation and show me the beauty of your face. Come, Lord Jesus, come. Amen.

—Unpublished Manuscript

Dear Lord Jesus,

How can I ever go anywhere else but to you to find the love I so desire! How can I expect from people as sinful as myself a love that can touch me in the most hidden corners of my being? Who can wash me clean as you do and give me food and drink as you do? Who wants me to be so close, so intimate, and so safe as you do? O Lord, your love is not an intangible love, a love that remains words and thoughts. No, Lord, your love is a love that comes from your human heart. It is a heart-felt love that expresses itself through your whole being. You speak ... you look ... you touch ... you give me food. Yes, you make your love a love that reaches all the senses of my body and holds me as a mother holds her child, embraces me as a father embraces his son, and touches me as a brother touches his sister and brother.

O dear Jesus, your heart is only love. I see you; I hear you; I touch you. With all my being, I know that you love me.

I trust in you, Lord, but keep helping me in my many moments of distrust and doubt. They are there and will be there every time I turn my eyes, ears, or hands away from you. Please, Lord, keep calling me back to you, by day and by night, in joy and in sadness, during moments of success and moments of failure. Never let me leave you. I know you walk with me. Help me walk with you today, tomorrow, and always.   —*Heart Speaks to Heart*

Good Friday

O dear Lord, what can I say to you on this holy night? Is there any word that could come from my mouth, any thought, any sentence? You died for me, you gave all for my sins, you not only became man for me but also suffered the most cruel death for me. Is there any response? I wish that I could find a fitting response, but in contemplating your Holy Passion and Death I can only confess humbly to you that the immensity of your divine love makes any response seem totally inadequate. Let me just stand and look at you. Your body is broken, your head wounded, your hands and feet are split open by nails, your side is pierced. Your dead body now rests in the arms of your Mother. It is all over now. It is finished. It is fulfilled. It is accomplished. Sweet Lord, gracious Lord, generous Lord, forgiving Lord, I adore you, I praise you, I thank you. You have made all things new through your passion and death. Your cross has been planted in this world as the new sign of hope.

Let me always live under your cross, O Lord, and proclaim the hope of your cross unceasingly. Amen.

—*A Cry for Mercy*

Easter Sunday

Dear Lord, risen Lord, light of the world, to you be all praise and glory! This day, so full of your presence, your joy, your peace, is indeed your day.

I just returned from a walk through the dark woods. It was cool and windy, but everything spoke of you. Everything: the clouds, the trees, the wet grass, the valley with its distant lights, the sound of the wind. They all spoke of your resurrection; they all made me aware that everything is indeed good. In you all is created good, and by you all creation is renewed and brought to an even greater glory than it possessed at its beginning.

As I walked through the dark woods at the end of this day, full of intimate joy, I heard you call Mary Magdalene by her name and heard how you called from the shore of the lake to your friends to throw out their nets. I also saw you entering the closed room where your disciples were gathered in fear. I saw you appearing on the mountain and at the outskirts of the village. How intimate these events really are. They are like special favors to dear friends. They were not done to impress or overwhelm anyone, but simply to show that your love is stronger than death.

O Lord, I know now that it is in silence, in a quiet moment, in a forgotten corner that you will meet me, call me by name and speak to me a word of peace. It is in my stillest hour that you become the risen Lord to me.

Dear Lord, I am so grateful for all you have given me this past week. Stay with me in the days to come. Bless all who suffer in this world and bring peace to your people, whom you loved so much that you gave your life for them. Amen.

— *A Cry for Mercy*

Pentecost

Dear Lord, listen to my prayer. You promised your disciples that you would not leave them alone but would send the Holy Spirit to guide them and lead them to the full Truth.

I feel like I am groping in the dark. I have received much from you, and still it is hard for me simply to be quiet and present in your presence. My mind is so chaotic, so full of dispersed ideas, plans, memories, and fantasies. I want to be with you and you alone, concentrate on your Word, listen to your voice, and look at you as you reveal yourself to your friends. But even with the best intentions I wander off to less important things and discover that my heart is drawn to my own little worthless treasures.

I cannot pray without the power from on high, the power of your Spirit. Send your Spirit, Lord, so that your Spirit can pray in me, can say "Lord Jesus," and can call out "Abba, Father."

I am waiting, Lord, I am expecting, I am hoping. Do not leave me without your Spirit. Give me your unifying and consoling Spirit. Amen.   —Unpublished Manuscript

Afterword

The Three Monks of Tolstoy

Three Russian monks lived on a faraway island. Nobody ever went there, but one day their bishop decided to make a pastoral visit. When he arrived he discovered that the monks didn't even know the Lord's Prayer. So he spent all his time and energy teaching them the "Our Father" and then left, satisfied with his pastoral work. But when his ship had left the island and was back in the open sea, he suddenly noticed the three hermits walking on the water — in fact, they were running after the ship! When they reached it they cried, "Dear Father, we have forgotten the prayer you taught us." The bishop, overwhelmed by what he was seeing and hearing, said, "But, dear brothers, how then do you pray?" They answered, "Well, we just say, 'Dear God, there are three of us and there are three of you, have mercy on us!'" The bishop, awestruck by their sanctity and simplicity, said, "Go back to your island and be at peace."   — *The Road to Daybreak*

Proceeds from the sale of this book will benefit the Dayspring at L'Arche Daybreak and the Henri Nouwen Society, which was founded to share "the spirituality of solitude, community, and compassion that was embodied in the life and ministry of Henri Nouwen."

We welcome readers to become "Friends" of the Henri Nouwen Society. For more information please visit the Henri Nouwen web site listed below or write to:

Henri Nouwen Society
P.O. Box 230523
Ansonia Station
New York, NY 10023 U.S.A.

For information about the Dayspring at L'Arche Daybreak, please write to:

Dayspring at L'Arche Daybreak
11339 Yonge Street
Richmond Hill, Ontario
Canada, L4S 1L1

For information about Henri's legacy, please visit the Henri Nouwen web site at http://www.hnlc.org.

Permissions

Acknowledgment is gratefully given for permission to reprint excerpts from the following works by Henri Nouwen:

BREAD FOR THE JOURNEY. Copyright © 1997 by Henri J. M. Nouwen. Reprinted by permission of HarperCollins Publishers, Inc.

CAN YOU DRINK THE CUP? Copyright © 1974 by Ave Maria Press, P.O. Box 428, Notre Dame, IN 46556. Used with permission of the publisher.

CLOWNING IN ROME. Copyright © 1979 by Henri J. M. Nouwen. Used by permission of Doubleday, a division of Random House, Inc.

COMPASSION (by Henri J. M. Nouwen, D. Morrison, and D. McNeill). Copyright © 1982 by Donald P. McNeill, Douglas A. Morrison, and Henri J. M. Nouwen. Used by permission of Doubleday, a division of Random House, Inc.

A CRY FOR MERCY. Copyright © 1981 by Henri J. M. Nouwen. Used by permission of Doubleday, a division of Random House, Inc.

THE GENESEE DIARY. Copyright © 1976 by Henri J. M. Nouwen. Used by permission of Doubleday, a division of Random House, Inc.

¡GRACIAS! A LATIN AMERICAN JOURNAL. Copyright © 1983 by Henri J. M. Nouwen. Reprinted by permission of HarperCollins Publishers, Inc.

HEART SPEAKS TO HEART. Copyright © 1989 by Ave Maria Press, P.O. Box 428, Notre Dame, IN 46556. Used with permission of the publisher.

IN MEMORIAM. Copyright © 1980 by Ave Maria Press, P.O. Box 428, Notre Dame, IN 46556. Used with permission of the publisher.

THE INNER VOICE OF LOVE. Copyright © 1996 by Henri Nouwen. Used by permission of Doubleday, a division of Random House, Inc.

Permissions

WITH OPEN HANDS. Copyright © 1974 by Ave Maria Press, P.O. Box 428, Notre Dame, IN 46556. Used with permission of the publisher.

THE WOUNDED HEALER. Copyright © 1972 by Henri J. M. Nouwen. Used by permission of Doubleday, a division of Random House, Inc.

Acknowledgment is gratefully extended to Sue Mosteller, C.S.J., Henri Nouwen's Literary Executrix, for permission to quote from the following articles:

"Anchored in God through Prayer." *Sojourners* 7 (April 1978): 20–21.

"Compassion: The Core of Spiritual Leadership" (with Donald McNeill and Douglas Morrison). *Worship Jubilee* 51 (January 1977): 22–23.

"Contemplation and Action," a sermon preached at St. Paul's Church, Columbia University, New York City. December 10, 1978.

"Discipleship and Reconciliation," an interview with Henri Nouwen. *Pax Christi*, USA, Winter 1991.

"The Duet of the Holy Spirit: When Mourning and Dancing Are One." *New Oxford Review* (June 1992): 5–12.

"Forgiveness: The Name of Love in a Wounded World." *Weavings* 7, no. 2 (March/April 1992): , 6–15.

"Intimacy, Fecundity and Ecstasy." *Radix* (May/June 1984): 8–23.

"Letting Go of All Things." *Sojourners* (May 1979): 5–6

"Parting Words: A Conversation on Prayer with Henri Nouwen." *Fellowship in Prayer* 47, no. 6 (December 1996): 6–20.

"Prayer and Ministry: An Interview with Henri Nouwen." *Sisters Today* (February 1977): 345–55.

"Prayer and Peacemaking." *Catholic Agitator* (December 1982): 4–5.

"Prayer and the Jealous God." *New Oxford Review* 52, no. 5 (June 1985): 7–12.

"Prayer Embraces the World." *Maryknoll Magazine* (April 1985): 17–21.

"A Quality of Heart: Henri Nouwen on Ministry, Suffering, Solitude, Activism and Prayer," an interview with John Garvey. *Notre Dame Magazine* (December 1981).

"Reborn from Above." *Spiritual Life* (Spring 1992): 29–32.

"Solitude and Community." *Worship* 52 (January 1978): 13–23.

"Spiritual Direction." *Worship* 55, no. 5 (September 1981): 399–404.

"A Spirituality of Waiting: Being Alert to God's Presence in Our Lives." *Weavings* 2, no. 1 (January–February, 1987): 6–17.

"Training for the Campus Ministry." *Pastoral Psychology* 20 (March 1969): 27–38.